INTRODUCTION

The adage 'if it ain't broke don't fix it' must be the maxim that the United States applies when naming a tank after General George Patton. The name was given to all future versions of this tank as we shall see in this short history of the M48 Patton tank.

The United States Armoured Corps ended the Second World War with several variations of tanks and were still labouring over the types: light, medium and heavy. This would soon be clarified by the use of the term MBT (Main Battle Tank). Although America, like most nations, was war weary and hoping for a long period of peace, it was also astute enough to realize that its armoured formations needed updating. Their main tank was still the venerable Sherman, which for all its faults, and its German nickname 'Tommy Cooker', had served the Allies well with its ease of production and sheer numbers produced. However, it was no match for the German Tiger and Panther (except for the British Firefly version armed with the efficient 17-pounder gun). So a heavy tank was designed and brought into service, the M26 Pershing, a celebrated American First World War general. After the war production of the M26 continued and a total of 2,500 were eventually produced. Like most tanks it went through improvements during its life and formed the basis for trials of different equipment. The shortcomings of the M26 were becoming obvious though and it would not be fit for soldiering in the future with the rapid advances of armour and main armament weapons, so plans for a new tank commenced.

The new tank was originally designated M26E2 Medium Tank Full Tracked. This was changed as it was felt that leaving the M26 as part of the nomenclature would simply infer a development of the M26. It was redesignated M40 sometime in 1948. Permission was given to build pilot tanks and by mid-November 1949 sixteen pilots had been produced and it was again redesignated: M46, still classed as a medium tank. The intention was that the M46 would be more mobile than the M26 and to that end the armour protection and armament was largely unchanged. Testing was carried out at the Aberdeen Proving Ground and at Fort Knox from December 1949 through to April 1950, and as trials are meant to do, two major failings were found. First was a disappointing lack of reliability, which is not a good thing for a vehicle designed to be on the front line. Second was a steering issue. Although alarming at first it was rectified and the steering improved. The Detroit tank factory was soon fulfilling the army's order for several hundred M46s, producing them at a rate of a dozen a day. The design was given a boost in 1950 when the United States president at the time, Harry S Truman, gave authorization for funding to increase the expansion of the tank programme.

This is the medium tank M26 Pershing that the United States finished the Second World War with. (Wiki Commons)

The next in line, the M47. From this side view the lineage from which the M48 sprang is evident. (Ulrich Wede Prime Portal)

This version of the M47 has done away with the small tensioner wheel at the rear. It would reappear on the M48, then disappear only to return a third time. (Brent Sauer Prime Portal)

The M46 found itself in combat during the Korean War, where its main adversary was the venerable Russian-supplied T-34. On 8 August 1950 the 6th Tank Battalion landed in South Korea and although the M46 proved its superiority over both versions of the T-34, it was used – as were the British Centurions – in fixed defensive positions in an artillery role. The M46 was popular with the crews in Korea and although the 90mm gun was inferior to the 20-pounder mounted on Centurion it was still a formidable weapon. The reliability issues were still there as the cooling system was not up to the hot dusty Korean weather. The M46 was leased free of charge to some European armies including Italy, Belgium and France. Crews got experience on the next tank that was to hit the inventory, the M47.

Above: This shows the long overhang of the turret bustle, and importantly for British Chieftain crews, the large bin secured to the rear. With Chieftain in Germany most M47s were used as hard targets and these bins were salvaged by the British tank crews to increase their stowage. (Brent Sauer Prime Portal)

Centre: An overhead view of T48, notice that the catwalks are devoid of stowage. Prominent is the cross-turret rangefinder and the commander's original cupola with the vision periscopes protruding above the rim. (Suzanne Marie Skurds M48 Interest Group)

Bottom: A common sight in the early days of the Cold War: American tanks deployed to face their Soviet opponents, seen here, at the famous Checkpoint Charlie in Berlin. The picture provides a good view of the early M48 rear hull, before it gained the twin-louvered doors. (M48 Appreciation Society)

It was accepted that the M46 programme had been rushed and was the result of an operational requirement and would need replacing. In its final form the M46 weighed in at 44 metric tons, had a length of 8.48m (27.82ft), mounted a 90mm gun with a .50-calibre Browning for the commander and a .30-calibre coaxial and .30-calibre Browning machine gun for the bow gunner in a ball mount in the glacis plate. The next in line was supposed to be the T42 (T denotes trials), and by June 1949 the wooden mock-up was ready. It was conventional in appearance with a four-man crew. The co-driver position was eliminated and it was not short of secondary armament. Besides the Browning mounted as coaxial machine gun, the commander had a .50-calibre Browning, the co-driver had a .30-calibre Browning and there were two further .30-calibre Brownings in blisters on either side of the turret. The project ended with the outbreak of the Korean War and as the tank was not developed sufficiently it was dropped. Six pilots had been constructed and it had played its part in the eventual development of the M48.

In 1950 the United States Army had to decide: should it carry on with the M26/M46 production, which, although there were problems, was a familiar vehicle to the crews? The resulting decision was not quite what was expected: the turret of the T42 was married to the hull of the M46. Even more bizarre the new tank was ordered into production. The actual production had its difficulties: the requirement for a new engine and electrics meant modification to the hulls; the production of 90mm guns was lagging behind the tank production and rangefinders, which had been introduced, were also in short supply. The decision was taken to issue the first tanks without rangefinders which would be retrospectively fitted as they became available. The new tank, consisting of the T42 turret on the modified hull, was then designated M47. In March 1952 firing trials were at last carried out with rangefinder-fitted tanks and overall were successful. In April 1952 the army formally accepted the M47.

The tank was 8.5m (27.88ft) long, weighed 48.5 tons, had a crew of five and was armed with a 90mm (3.5in) main armament with 70 rounds, a .50-calibre M2 (12.7mm) for the commander and a .30-calibre coaxial machine gun and .30-calibre (7.62mm) Browning M1919A4 for the bow gunner. The M47 never saw action in service with the United States but certainly did with many other countries. Although many thousands were produced it was replaced quite quickly in the American inventory by the M48. Foreign users included Belgium, Pakistan, Jordan, Turkey, Brazil, Greece and the then South Vietnam. Many of these users adapted the tanks to suit their own doctrine, which included some strange adaptations. One such was produced by

the United Kingdom who, although not a user, put forward several ideas to adapt M47s to various roles, one of these involved fitting the British Aircraft Corporation Swingfire long-range guided missile to the turret, with a twin launcher on either side: nothing came of this.

Although the M47 concept worked, issues were evident even before it went into full production. The major one was its protection; it was felt that the protection of the turret was weaker than its hull, not an ideal situation. In fact, work had begun on its replacement even while M47 was being accepted. The new tank design was being worked on by the Detroit Tank Arsenal and given the designation T48.

Detroit's design study had been accepted by the army and on 8 December 1950 a contract to design and manufacture Tank 90mm T48 was given to the Chrysler Corporation. Six pilots were produced by Chrysler by the end of 1951 and were first shown to the public on 1 July 1952. In a typical showmanship event the tank burst through a paper screen and drove into, and snapped, telegraph poles. That day the widow of General George Patton named the tank 'Patton' in his memory.

The most noticeable change to the design was the turret. It was rather like an upturned frying pan, similar to the Russian T-54/55 design, but much bigger.

The army still had a tank mounting a 90mm gun, but now with a crew of four, as the hull gunner had been removed allowing a much better ballistic-hull shape. This tank was to serve the United States very well, and was developed into several variants and specialized armour, even once it had left American service it could be found in use in several armies worldwide.

The final development of the series, although never officially called a Patton – rather as a product-improved version of the Patton series – was the M60. During the Hungarian revolution the British were gifted, in a most dramatic way, a close up look inside and out of the current

A typical scene in Germany: the Germans became very stoic about tanks moving through their towns, especially in the early days of the Cold War, and the damage they caused. Notice the rubber burn marks where the tanks have manoeuvred. Two M48A1s and a military policeman seem to have things under control. (Suzanne Marie Skuda M48 Appreciation Society)

Soviet tank: the T-54A. It was driven into the grounds of the British embassy by Hungarian patriots. As can be imagined,

An M48 slowly makes its way up a very steep hill, showing just what inclines it can tackle, albeit slowly. This is not an ideal approach when in combat as the whole lower hull is exposed to enemy fire, and the hull bottom is always the weakest part on most tanks. (M48 Appreciation Society)

the Russians were jumping up and down demanding the return of their tank. The British of course complied, slowly, first allowing their experts to amass as much information on the tank as could be obtained in a short time.

Some of the information was over exaggerated, possibly not a bad thing as it makes the counter design that much more effective. One outcome was the design by the British of the 105mm tank gun to replace the 20-pounder then in use. Information gained was shared with the Americans. One outcome was the adoption, under licence, of the L7 105mm tank gun for what would be their next tank, the M60.

That tank was officially designated M60 in March 1959. By the time it left service 15,000 M60s had been built by Chrysler. Like most main battle tanks the M60 went through many updates during its life; using an interior based on the M48 gave plenty of room for these upgrades. Many NATO allies also used it and many still have it in front-line service, including Egypt and Saudi Arabia.

This then gives us a brief overview of the origins of the Patton family of tanks.
The M48 was certainly no game changer for design, but it brought in many features

M48 Patton in Detail

A side view of a M48A1 spending its days at a military museum in the United States. Note the multi-coloured camouflage and the small tension wheel at the rear. (M48 Appreciation Society)

to improve the lot of American tank crew members. The layout was conventional, in that for a crew of four, the driver was located centrally in the hull. This location was used as the removal of the bow gunner/co-driver gave more space and it is the most sensible location for the driver of the tank. The three remaining crew members are all located in the turret, with the loader/operator located on the left and the gunner on the right, below the commander who is located with his own cupola on the right. Although there are variations of the M48, the description is applicable, unless otherwise mentioned, to all the gun tanks.

The Hull
The hull of the M48 was quite a departure from previous American tanks in that the castings produced quite a graceful shape compared with the M47 and the British Centurion. These were both still very angular in their appearance. It was also a major breakaway from the slab-sided tanks of the previous decade of which the Sherman is a prime example. This is apparent in the design of the hull bottom which had, for a long time in most nations' tanks, been flat, which was a great help for building but of little use ballistically,

leaving the bottom exposed to damage and penetration by landmines.

It had been known that sloping armour would help defeat this sort of problem but applying it to a hull bottom was an issue. The M48's designers tried to alleviate this by making the hull bottom rounded, it joined the upper hull which was also a round shape. The front edge of the glacis had a very distinctive boat-shaped edge to it as a result of the two round parts of the hull needing to be bevelled to ensure a good join.

The hull was an armour casting, which was quite an achievement for that period as most tanks were built-up of welded plates with smaller castings, such as a turret. The designers tried to minimize the amount of openings that had to be included in the hull, as all openings weaken the overall structure strength. However, holes for the torsion bar suspension, access plates and drain plate covers all had to be included.

The hull was effectively divided into two major spaces with a bulkhead separating the rear areas from the turret space and driver's area. The rear part of the hull contained the Continental AV-1790 engine, coupled to an Allison CD-850-4 transmission. A GM A41-1 auxiliary engine was fitted in the front left corner of the engine bay. This was used to power a 240-volt generator that could provide power for the tank's services without the need to run the main engine when in a tactical location, and to help keep the batteries at full charge. The main fuel tanks were also located in this compartment. It was covered by a series of louvered engine and transmission decks. The louvres allowed the flow of air to help cool the engine. One weaker design feature was that the location of the fuel tanks was on either side of the engine, which posed a problem when refuelling with petrol. It was also a tedious process as the right fuel tank could only accept fuel at a rate of 25 gallons per minute. As the tanks were interlinked this tended to slow the process. The fuel tanks could hold 215 gallons of which 200 gallons was useable.

The tank rode on torsion bar suspension. Although it gave a fairly stable ride, it had the knock-on effect of raising the tank's overall height. As the bars ran from one side of the tank to the other, the hull and turret floors were that much higher than if the suspension was bolted to the outside. This in turn meant the hull and turret were increased in size; this was always a feature taught in vehicle recognition classes: the height of American tanks compared with Western allies and even more so to the Soviets' tanks. It had six road wheels per side and the track was supported by five top rollers with shock absorbers fitted to the first, second and sixth road wheel stations. Due to the use of torsion bars the road wheels are not in line left and right. A stagger of three to four inches accommodates the torsion bars.

American National Guard using M48A5s for training at Fort Drum in 1981. Notice that both commander and loader have 7.62mm machine guns. (M48 Appreciation Society)

An M48 in its natural environment. This image shows the upper and lower castings and the rounded effect where the upper and lower glacis join. This is probably a M48 of the Bundeswehr, judging by the German-style smoke grenade launchers fitted. Notice also the T-blast deflector; it is also fitted with the much-unloved M1 cupola. (Ulrich Wede Prime Portal)

The right-hand headlight set from a M48A5. The yellow sign covered in masking tape is the bridge classification sign telling the crew what weight bridge can safely be crossed. Notice the hooded sidelight above and between the two main lights. (Erik Tops Prime Portal)

The early deck of the M48. Notice the location of the gun travelling clamp and the turret basket. (M48 Appreciation Society)

This is the rear of an early M48 before the new engine programme. Notice the engine decks and the hull rear, and compare it to the M48A2. (Prime Portal)

This view is of the engine decks of the M48A2. Notice the difference the AV-1790-8 fuel-injected engine makes; instead of louvered decks right across, they are now only on the side of the compartment. The central portion is raised to accommodate the new engine. The slope of the hull can be seen quite clearly here as well. (David Luck Prime Portal)

The track was adjusted by means of the idler wheel located at the front of the tank, this could tighten or slacken the track as required. Later on a small jockey wheel was fitted at the rear in an attempt to reduce the incidence of thrown tracks. Drive was taken from the rear-mounted sprockets; the track was joined together by end connectors, as can be seen in the current British Challenger 2 tank. Catwalks were fitted either side over the tracks with stowage bins fitted to these, along with some of the tools. The top run of the track was covered by track guards and as these were only sheet metal the M48 can often be seen on exercise or operations minus these items. A gun travelling lock was located at the rear of the hull and an infantry tank telephone was locate on the right of the hull rear plate. This device allowed the infantry to talk directly to the crew in the tank when the crew was operating closed down. This was a slightly better location than the British who seem to favour it located on the hull rear wall, which can be disconcerting to the infantry if the tank decides to move in reverse.

The driver's controls were all to hand and reasonably easy to operate, although new or unwary drivers have been known to select reverse gears on the automatic gear box selector lever. Instead of going into low range the tank would produce loud mechanic noises as the gear box tried to select reverse while still moving forward. This is a mistake only made once. The driver steered the vehicle by means of an aircraft-type steering wheel, the transmission selector lever was located by his right side. When the driver was operating closed-down he was provided with three T25 periscopes which gave him roughly 180 degrees of forward vision. His means of access was via a swinging hatch, which in late models was changed to a heavier lift-and-swing version. The T25 periscopes dropped down when the hatch was opened on the earlier small hatches. On later tanks infra-red night-driving periscopes were mounted in the hatch. One other feature of the driver's cab was the escape hatch, which by means of pulling a lever released the hatch, and operating another allowed him to swing his seat to one side and exit the vehicle. Service in Vietnam showed this to be a weak feature when the tank hit anti-tank mines, so bars were welded to the outside. This prevented the hatch from being blown into the cab and injuring the driver. The bars were welded across the bottom but still allowed the driver to drop the hatch in an emergency.

The Turret

The turret was deemed very spacious in comparison to previous American tanks. The whole turret was one casting which gave an armour thickness ranging from 176mm (7in) at the front of the turret to 54mm (2.5in) at the rear. There was plenty

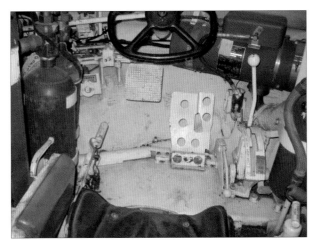

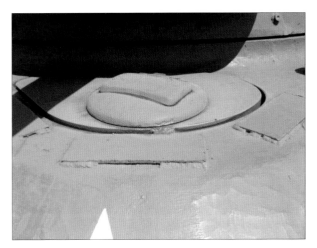

The driver's compartment in a M48A5. Note the central driver's seat and the gear selector lever on the right; the accelerator and brake pedals are in their normal locations. The driver also shares the cab with two fixed fire extinguishers. At the top of the picture the aircraft-style steering wheel can be seen; the cab is painted white, as is common in American tanks. (Wiki commons)

Although their apertures have been plated over, the three driver's periscopes and the location in the hatch for the infra-red driving sight would indicate that this is the late hatch giving the driver just a bit more room to gain entry and exit.

This shows the pop-up feature of one of the driver's three periscopes for closed-down driving. (Ulrich Wede Prime Portal)

This picture shows how the sprocket wheel picks up the track. This is similar to how the current British Challenger 2 is laid out. Previously the sprocket teeth engaged slots on the inside of the track. (Suzanne Marie Skurds M48 Interest Group)

of room in the turret for the remaining three crew members: the driver was in a sense isolated down in the front of the vehicle.

The loader is located on the left side of the turret and, as in all tanks with a loader, probably has the most space to move around in. His duties are many and varied. He is responsible for loading the coaxial machine gun and for ensuring that any stoppages are cleared quickly. He also has responsibility for loading the 90mm gun. This fires either HEAT (High Explosive Anti-Tank) or HVAP (High Velocity Armour Piercing) rounds. The latter is similar to the British APDS (Armour Piercing Discarding Sabot) rounds. In these rounds a solid core of a dense material, usually tungsten, is contained in a lightweight carrier which falls away once the round leaves the muzzle. However, HVAP retains the outer carrier which is far more effective than the older armour-piercing round which fired a solid shot the same diameter as the bore. Other natures that could be used depending on the tactical situation

A good overhead view useful for detailing showing the loader's hatch on a M48A5. Notice that there is nothing fancy like torsion bars to tension the hatch, simply two springs. This might be an issue if they were blown off by shrapnel; it might make opening the hatch just a bit more difficult. (Erik Torp Prime Portal)

Although dismounted from the vehicle this gives a good idea of the 90mm gun and the associated fittings. Centre of the image are the groves in the breech ring in which the vertical sliding breech block moves. To the left is the coaxial .30-calibre Browning; note to the right of it the remote cocking handle, as the loader could not reach the normal one in this position. (Suzanne Marie Skurds M48 Interest Group)

A M48A2 in a German tank museum. In front are the types of ammunition that could be fired from the 90mm gun. Mounted on the top of the barrel is the German gunfire sound and flash simulator. When the gunner fired one of these cartridges from the main gun, instead of a 90mm round, it makes the sound and gives off the smoke flash to simulate gunfire. There were many versions in use in different armies in the late 1970s. The British used one called Simfire, but they took a lot of setting up and were often inoperative. (Tank Encyclopaedia)

Ammunition stowage in part of a M48 turret. Note the box to the right marked binoculars. Armies use boxes like this with clear labels; once in service the crew would stow items where they felt they were most useful, and the boxes would be utilized to hold other items. (M48 Appreciation Society)

were smoke and canister. Canister is a very effective anti-personnel round and in its simplest form could be likened to a 90mm shotgun cartridge. It is loaded with steel balls and is fired at close range: the balls spread out in a lethal pattern. The Australians in Vietnam made great use of this, firing 20-pounder canister to break up Viet Cong attacks. The ammunition for the 90mm gun was stored in racks around the turret ring as well as two racks next to the driver and a rack under the gun. The loader's other main job was to ensure that the tank's radios were fully operational and when deployed always maintained a listening watch. He would send and receive messages which helped take the load off the commander who had enough to do just running the vehicle.

The gunner and commander both occupy the right-hand side of the turret with the gunner sitting below the commander. He is equipped with a twin handle directly in line with his lap. Using this he can control the hydraulic motors that provide turret traverse and elevation of the 90mm and coaxial machine gun. This is in stark contrast to the British who preferred the electric drive for gun and turret, with the view that if the turret was penetrated no hot hydraulic fluid would be sprayed about. The gunner also had hand controls to traverse and elevate the gun. His firing control allowed him to fire the main armament and the machine gun electrically. In the event of a malfunction he could also fire them manually. The installation of fire-control equipment appears to be a bit haphazard, probably because when production started they were fitted with whatever was to hand. Some early vehicles were fitted with a similar arrangement to that found in the M47 tank; this was not an ideal way to introduce the new vehicle. A good example of how jargon can conjure misleading mental images is the statement that the M48 was fitted with a ballistic fire-control computer. This sounds fantastic until you realize that the T30 ballistic computer was only a mechanical analogue device which added the elevation to the gunner's M20 periscope; information on the type of ammunition was added using the ballistic drive. Although very basic, it was a step forward and showed where fire-control solutions were heading; it just needed the technology to catch up. The gunner probably had the most cramped seat in the tank and once the commander was in position there was very little room to move, despite the generous dimensions of the turret. In the event of the tank being hit, there was always a concern that the gunner might not be able to get past an incapacitated commander.

The final member of the crew is the vehicle commander, who is located on the right side of the turret, above the gunner. The cupola fitted will depend on the version of M48 he is commanding. The original cupola was quite low in profile and gave

Although this turret looks as if it has been in the wars it is what the Americans call a Tower Turret Trainer. Similar ideas were used by the British and called Classroom Instructional Models. Basically they are a frame with large cut-outs that allow students to see the components. Some versions have operational working parts so that accurate training can take place. Clearly visible is the breech ring containing the vertically sliding breech block. Also note the linkage from the commander's controls running down to the gunner's location. (Dieter Krause Prime Portal)

him plenty of room; it was equipped with four plastic M17 periscopes to give him all-round vision when closed down. His seat was adjustable and could be folded to allow him to either sit with his head out, stand, or sit fully closed down. The commander's cupola mounted a .50-calibre machine gun and could be fired either from inside the turret or from outside. Later versions of M48 had the M1 cupola which enclosed the .50-calibre machine gun. While this allowed the commander to reload the weapon under cover, space constraints reduced the ready amount of ammunition. Access to the M1 cupola was from a rearward opening hatch. The cupola was equipped with vison blocks instead of periscopes for all-round vision and a periscopic sight for firing the machine gun. The use of the M1 cupola led to a 1ft height increase of the tank. In service the M1 cupola was highly unpopular. Some M48s were fitted with what was known as a Model 30 cupola, which was developed by Aircraft Armaments Incorporated and would become a hallmark of the M48 series.

Once the commander had acquired a target that he wished to engage, he had to find the range to it using the T46E1 rangefinder. This was cross-turret mounted in front of his position. Apart from this the commander has to be situation aware and constantly checking the ground ahead, issuing instructions and map reading. All this makes the commander's role incredibly labour intensive.

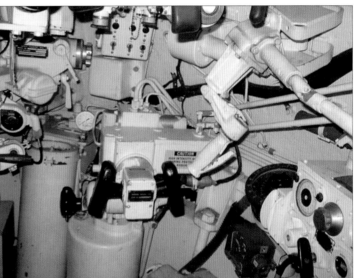

The gunner's position in a M48A5; there is not much difference in the gunner's position in the different marks. In front can be seen the gunner's traverse and elevation controls: incline left and the turret goes left and vice versa; rotate toward you and the gun goes up; push it away and the gun goes down. (M48 Appreciation Society)

Another view of the Tower Turret Trainer. This time the loader's hatch is visible. The cross-turret rangefinder can clearly be seen as can the interior of the M1 cupola. (Dieter Krause Prime Portal)

This picture shows just how much space the body of the .50-calibre Browning takes up in the M1 cupola. The trunking is for empty cases and links, as the ammunition is joined together by metal links which are stripped off as the weapon loads. A superior method to the old-style cloth ammunition belts. (Paul Clarkson)

It seems that even in a tank the crew are not spared an overwhelming amount of warning signs. Here the signs warn the crew not to traverse until all members are clear of moving parts. The green box is one of the radio harnesses, and as can be seen on its face, it gives the user several setting options. (Wiki Commons)

Centre left: This illustrates just how awkward getting into the M1 cupola was. This poor Bundeswehr soldier is struggling and he has all the time in the world; image if it was in action and the tank had been hit and both the commander and gunner are trying to escape in a hurry. (Suzanne Marie Skurds M48 Interest Group)

This view from, the front of the M1 cupola, shows the size of it. One can only wonder just how effective those vision blocks were. (Dieter Krause prime Portal)

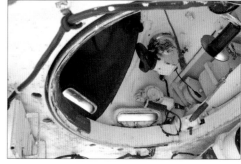

Looking up into the M1 cupola, the commander's sight eyepiece is visible in the centre. Although it was cramped at least it did have some vision devices to aid the commander. (Dieter Krause Prime Portal)

Bottom left: From the Tower Turret Trainer showing the commander's position and his power control handle. Also visible is the eyepiece for the cross-turret rangefinder, the interior of the M1 cupola which seems very spacious without the .50-calibre Browning, and the vision block on the left of the cupola: its limited view is apparent. (Dieter Hause Prime Portal)

M48 Main Battle Tank Variants

The M48 produced many variants on its hull, and these included not only different versions of the tank but also specialized equipment for engineers and artillery. Like most armoured vehicles, once the M48 entered service, various modifications were found to be required to make the vehicle more useable. This is not a reflection on poor design but simply user experience that often shows up issues not found during trials. To an outsider some may seem very minor, such as moving a mounting bracket a few inches, but if this is your office for some time, that move could prevent serious injury. One bizarre trial carried out was subjecting three M48s to a nuclear blast. Positioned 500 yards from the blast, all three survived in varying states of damage. After some repairs two were drivable but not fightable as rangefinders and all sights had been knocked out of calibration. Although it showed what the tank could withstand this was not a common test and although the vehicles survived the crews would have died from radiation poisoning in a real-life situation.

Once the M48 was standardized there were three versions in service. One version had the original cupola and the small driver's hatch previously mentioned; the second had the same cupola with a large driver's hatch; and the third had the large driver's hatch coupled with the Model 30 cupola. The first became the standard M48 while the second became the M48A1, as did version three once it had the cupolas changed to the Model 30. These designations only lasted for around 20 months when the decision to adopt the M48A1 as the standard tank was made and to relegate the M48.

The M48A1 went into full production at the Chrysler works in 1955–6. By then a total of 1,800 tanks had been produced and supplied to the army, who would use them until the mid-1970s when they were replaced by M48A3s. Apart from the modifications already listed, the M48A1 stayed very much the same until it was superseded.

The next in line was the M48A2 which was designed partially to rectify one of the big issues with the M48A1: its infra-red signature. At times it was so bad that besides giving away the tank's location it was so obvious it could actually be identified as an M48A1. No mean feat given the state of the infra-red equipment then in

Brand new, straight from the factory: this line-up of M48A1s parade in front of VIPs and dignitaries. (Mark Holloway M48 Appreciation Society)

A troop or section of M48A1s looking as if they have arrived at, or are just leaving, a tank range in what may well be Germany. Notice the small tension wheel at the rear and the prominent call sign painted in yellow. (Michael Kalbfleisch Prime Portal)

Notice how the rear view has changed with the fitting of the new engine; the top decks have been modified and there are two large louvered doors instead of a fixed rear plate. This design worked so well it was carried forward to the M60 programme. (Prime Portal)

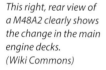

This right, rear view of a M48A2 clearly shows the change in the main engine decks. (Wiki Commons)

use. When the M48 was developed, night fighting was not really an issue and not too much thought was given to it. The use of simple infra-red equipment by the Soviets in their emerging T-54s brought the issue to the fore. Even the British ran trials to minimize the heat signature from the Conqueror which, considering its size, was a challenge.

The M48A2 had a completely redesigned engine compartment which allowed the fuel capacity to be improved by up to 50 percent. This went some way to alleviating the M48's small operational range.

The other major change was the substitution of the Continental AV-1790-5 air-cooled engine for the fuel-injected Continental AV-1790-8. The injector was in fact British; the rights to build it in America had been obtained from the SU Company who had provided the fuel injectors for the Conqueror's fuel-injected Meteor engine. It was hoped that the fitting of this would help improve the operational range. In fact, an increase of around 45 miles was claimed. Looking at the tank from the outside the engine compartment was now squarer in

shape. The exhaust was moved from the centre of the decks and was now vented via the two large louvered doors that were part of the hull rear.

The logic behind this was that instead of the heat being contained in a small area, as in the early exhaust, it was spread over a much larger area via the doors. It was hoped this would help to lower the infra-red signature. The tank telephone was moved from the rear and relocated on the right-hand track guard. The new engine compartment seems to have been successful as it was – in slightly modified form – carried over to the M60 series. It was also used by most countries that acquired the M48 when they came to carry out their own hull upgrades. Fire-control equipment was modified by fitting the M13A1 stereoscopic rangefinder instead of the original M13 version, and improvements to the mountings enabled them to stand up to the constant stress of the 90mm recoil. Changes to the fire-control system also included the fitting of an electro-hydraulic control system which allowed both gunner and commander to traverse and elevate the gun. This made

An M48A2C spending its retirement in the sun, with a nice fresh coat of paint. The studs that held the canvas cover that would have been fitted over the mantlet can be clearly seen. (Wiki Commons)

it much easier for a commander to lay the gunner onto the target he wished to engage, instead of trying to do it by target description. In theory, the target should appear within the gunner's eyepiece. However, compared to the British Centurion the M48A1 still had no stabilization fitted, which limited engagements on the move. The stereoscopic rangefinder was changed again in the M48A2C. It was replaced with a coincidence rangefinder which uses mechanical and optical principles to allow an operator to determine the distance to a visible object: this allows the commander to read off the range. One way to distinguish the M48A2, besides the cupola and the very distinctive engine decks, is that it only had three top rollers as opposed to the five on previous versions. This was done in an effort to reduce all-up weight and was taken a stage further in the M48A2C when the small track tensioning idler, located at the sprocket end of the hull, was also removed.

Night fighting was still very much in its infancy as technology was still experimenting with ways of being able to view the enemy in the dark without being seen. Infra-red sights were available but were not sufficiently advanced to allow accurate designation, important if blue-on-blue contact was to be avoided. So for the time being white light was the only method available, and to that end 2kw searchlights were available to be fitted. This was mounted on the mantlet giving it the same degree of movement that the gun had. It was in an unarmoured box which is a distinct disadvantage in combat. It was possible to fit an infra-red filter on it but the only optic that could view this was the driver's night-driving periscope and the commander's binoculars.

Production of the M48A2 began in 1956 and ended in 1959 to allow for the commencement of the M60 program. During this time 11,703 M48A2s had been produced, although many were not for the

A typical posed image, often produced for publicity and recruiting. Note the headlight arrangement and the fact that the inner headlight of each set has an infra-red lens fitted. (M48 Appreciation Society)

This image shows how the searchlight was mounted to the mantlet on the M48. When not in use it could be removed and fitted into a stowage box located on the turret rear. (Mark Clarkson)

The bane of any tank crew's life: the 100 percent tool checks. Every item of equipment is laid out and checked by a unit's technical staff. Deficiencies will be billed to the individual while damaged items will be replaced. Until the kit is laid out, as in the picture, it cannot be appreciated just how much equipment a tank has to carry. For some items this is the only time they will see the light of day as they are considered so useless by the crew they will stay on a shelf in the troop stores. (Carl Tarrant Prime Portal)

The birthplace of M48s: the Chrysler Tank Factory in Delaware. Although not as fast as an automobile assembly line the principle is the same. At each stage something is fitted by a team whose main job will just be those components. (Nikos Hatzitsiru Prime Portal)

United States Army but for foreign countries, where some are still in use. Some ended up with nations not friendly toward America but using captured tanks, the Democratic Republic of Vietnam being a good example. Tanks also found their way to nations that the United States would not usually supply arms to as it was almost impossible to prevent the resale of this equipment in former combat zones especially since the tanks were old and in the process of being replaced. As such it was hardly worth chasing up the erring nations.

As we have seen, the introduction of the M60 programme signalled the end of M48 production, but further development of the type took place. One step taken was the total modernization of the very old and problematic M48A1s. They were rebuilt using M60 components which were readily available. These included the AVDS-1790 diesel engine, which meant new engine decks. The move to diesel came with the

realization that a diesel fleet of AFVs was a lot safer than using volatile petrol. This was not just the tanks but included all AFVs. The improved fire controls from the M48A2C were fitted to these vehicles and their final designation was M48A3: a long-serving variant.

The Browning machine gun was replaced by a 7.62mm gun, thus bringing the United States in line with the ammunition used by European nations. The resulting tanks were used to replace older M48s in units that were not yet scheduled to receive the M60. The benefits obtained by fitting a diesel engine was that at last an M48 variant had a decent combat range: now up to 300 miles. Noticeable on the track guard was the top-loading air filters required for the diesel engine. Also, just to confuse the AFV recognition buffs, the top rollers removed on conversion to M48A2 were now re-introduced. After experience with the Nuclear, Biological and Chemical (NBC) protection used on the M60 series it was decided to fit it to the M48A3 as well. Two units were provided, one for the driver and one for the turret crew, these provided fresh, filtered air to each crew member, a face mask was made available for them to wear too. One modification that was meant to improve life for the commander seems to have been somewhat ignored: after the removal of the hated M1 cupola, and the fitting of the low-profile cupola, they complained that it did not provide 360-degree coverage. To accommodate this an adaptor ring was fitted between the cupola and the turret, with eight vision blocks to give the required coverage. As most M48 crews preferred to operate with all hatches opened it may have been a wasted effort. The searchlight was now changed to the Zenon type with stowage located at the rear of the turret basket to stow it when not in use.

Left: A posed picture shows the commander's low profile cupola and the mounting in this case of a .30-calibre Browning. Note also how the ammunition box is retained in its holder. (M48 Appreciation Society)

Below: A solution to the M1 cupola, its cramped working conditions and lack of vision can be seen in this image. A riser was put under the M1 with better vision blocks. This partially helped as it raised the tank's profile even higher. (Wiki Commons)

The M48A1 was fitted with the M60 105mm gun instead of the long-serving 90mm, and was re-designated M48A1E1. Since the M48A3 had the M60 diesel engine installation as well as the 105mm gun it made sense to combine these features in a new version of the M48, the designation was M48A1E3. Thus an almost replica M60 was produced and the only way to distinguish the M60 from the M48A1E3 was by looking at the glacis plate join: the M60's was a sharp join while the M48's was rounded. It was proposed that the conversions completed so far should be designated M48A4. In the end the M48A4 never entered production. That was not the end of the M48 for a new, ambitious, forward-looking programme was planned for the series.

In the early 1970s the United States had more or less withdrawn all its M48s from front-line service, replacing them with the M60, with most of the M48A3s going to the National Guard. At this time there was also the futuristic programme between the United States and the then Federal Republic of Germany for the MBT70 project. This deserves a book of its own as it is a fascinating story, but the project eventually fell through and both countries went on to produce their own version of the tank, which failed to go into production. This left the United States with no new main battle tank on the drawing board or in production, which was a worrying state of affairs. The only way forward was to start again, eventually producing the M1 Abrams. The big worry at the time was a shortage of tanks due to large shipments being sent to Israel to replace their losses after the 1973 Arab-Israeli War which had cost Israel dearly in men and machines. Coupled with this was the growing strength of the Soviet Union tank forces and the fact that it was no longer possible to deride

Although this M48 now spends its days as a hard target, it does show several points to good advantage. These include the way the loader's hatch opens, the clamps holding the canvas mantlet cover on, the rangefinder blister and the total lack of vision devices on the cupola. It must have been a nightmare to operate with such limited vision. (M48 Appreciation Society)

their product as 'rough and ready' for the quality and innovation was improving every day. All this was causing great concern to the NATO chiefs of staff. What was needed a quick fix until the M60A1 programme produced enough tanks to fill the gap. It would be a long time until the M1 was ready to be fielded.

A posed group in front of an M48. It shows the side of the turret well as well as the uniforms of the troops posing. (M48 Appreciation Society)

Left: This M48A5 of the Bundeswehr will be of value when modelling the M48A5. Firstly, there is a good depiction of the German tank uniform, including their black beret. Secondly, the tank is fitted with the British weapon's effect simulator Simfire. Components that can be seen are the flash/bang generator on top of the turret behind the mantlet, and on either side forward of the turret are two of the detector units. These will pick up the laser beam from an opposing tank. Just visible at the rear is the rotary amber light which will flash when the vehicle is hit and knocked out. An optional smoke pot can also be ignited. The cables hanging down are part of the system as well. (Soris Kon)

amount of work required on it. Obviously the older tanks needed more work than the M48A3s. Refitting an M48A3 meant fitting the new gun and its associated ammunition, along with a new turret basket – the part that hangs down inside the turret that has all the crew turret seats and equipment fitted to it – which meant the loader did not have to follow the turret as the basket floor rotated with the turret – a much easier and safer option. New track was also fitted, along with the top-loader air cleaners from the M60. Early vehicles resorted to the unpopular M1 cupola fitted with the vision-riser block to improve viewing. Later versions had the Israeli Urdan low-profile cupola which was very similar to the original low-profile cupola from way back in the early days of M4 development. Approximately 2,050 conversions were carried out, and although it was a cheap fix in terms of getting tanks to the troops, the modified tanks served until such time as the M60 became available and the M1 Abrams took on the mantle of United States main battle tank.

Looking to the front left of the vehicle this picture shows how the commander's cupola sits slightly recessed. Note the location of the tow rope and lifting eyes. (Erik Torp Prime Portal)

We have seen how the M48 could accept the diesel engine and the licence-built British L7 105mm gun, so the decision was taken to bring mothballed M48s, M48A1s, M48A2s and almost all the M48A3s up to M60 standard. The resulting tanks would be known as M48A5s. Depending on which version was being rebuilt determined the

This then is the story of the M48 series of American tanks, from its inception through to its final days in service. It served on for many years in other nations and served as the basis for specialized armour utilizing

CONTINUES ON PAGE 48

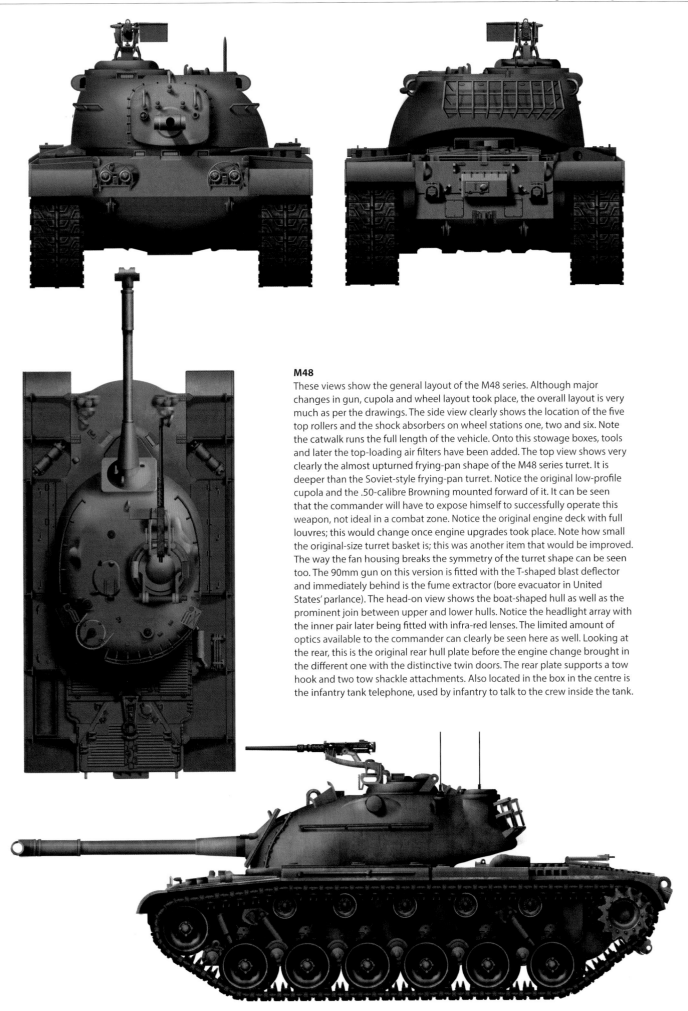

M48

These views show the general layout of the M48 series. Although major changes in gun, cupola and wheel layout took place, the overall layout is very much as per the drawings. The side view clearly shows the location of the five top rollers and the shock absorbers on wheel stations one, two and six. Note the catwalk runs the full length of the vehicle. Onto this stowage boxes, tools and later the top-loading air filters have been added. The top view shows very clearly the almost upturned frying-pan shape of the M48 series turret. It is deeper than the Soviet-style frying-pan turret. Notice the original low-profile cupola and the .50-calibre Browning mounted forward of it. It can be seen that the commander will have to expose himself to successfully operate this weapon, not ideal in a combat zone. Notice the original engine deck with full louvres; this would change once engine upgrades took place. Note how small the original-size turret basket is; this was another item that would be improved. The way the fan housing breaks the symmetry of the turret shape can be seen too. The 90mm gun on this version is fitted with the T-shaped blast deflector and immediately behind is the fume extractor (bore evacuator in United States' parlance). The head-on view shows the boat-shaped hull as well as the prominent join between upper and lower hulls. Notice the headlight array with the inner pair later being fitted with infra-red lenses. The limited amount of optics available to the commander can clearly be seen here as well. Looking at the rear, this is the original rear hull plate before the engine change brought in the different one with the distinctive twin doors. The rear plate supports a tow hook and two tow shackle attachments. Also located in the box in the centre is the infantry tank telephone, used by infantry to talk to the crew inside the tank.

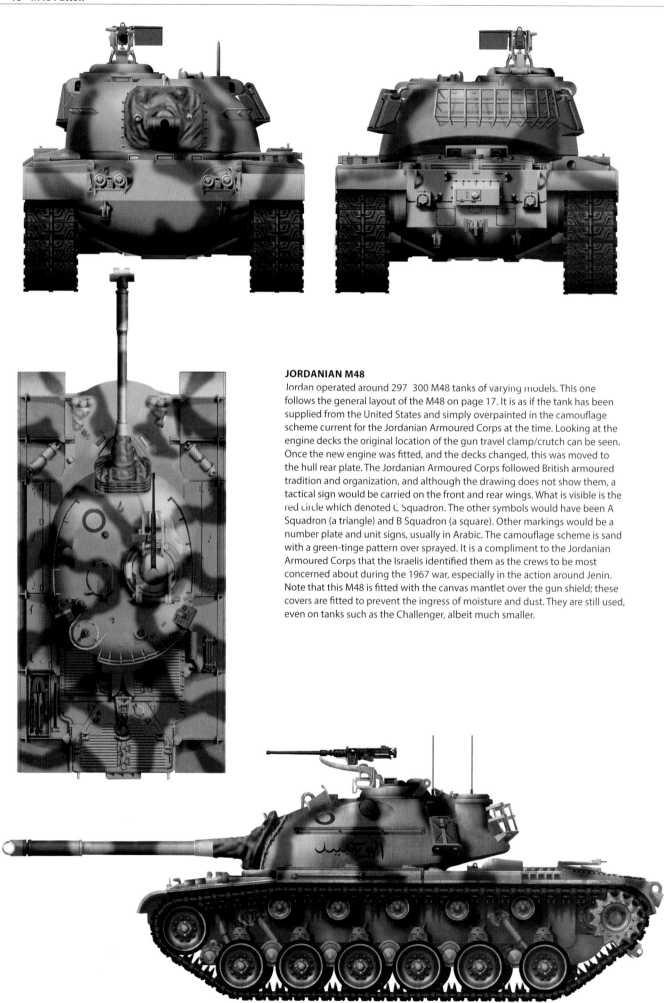

JORDANIAN M48

Jordan operated around 297 300 M48 tanks of varying models. This one follows the general layout of the M48 on page 17. It is as if the tank has been supplied from the United States and simply overpainted in the camouflage scheme current for the Jordanian Armoured Corps at the time. Looking at the engine decks the original location of the gun travel clamp/crutch can be seen. Once the new engine was fitted, and the decks changed, this was moved to the hull rear plate. The Jordanian Armoured Corps followed British armoured tradition and organization, and although the drawing does not show them, a tactical sign would be carried on the front and rear wings. What is visible is the red circle which denoted C Squadron. The other symbols would have been A Squadron (a triangle) and B Squadron (a square). Other markings would be a number plate and unit signs, usually in Arabic. The camouflage scheme is sand with a green-tinge pattern over sprayed. It is a compliment to the Jordanian Armoured Corps that the Israelis identified them as the crews to be most concerned about during the 1967 war, especially in the action around Jenin. Note that this M48 is fitted with the canvas mantlet over the gun shield; these covers are fitted to prevent the ingress of moisture and dust. They are still used, even on tanks such as the Challenger, albeit much smaller.

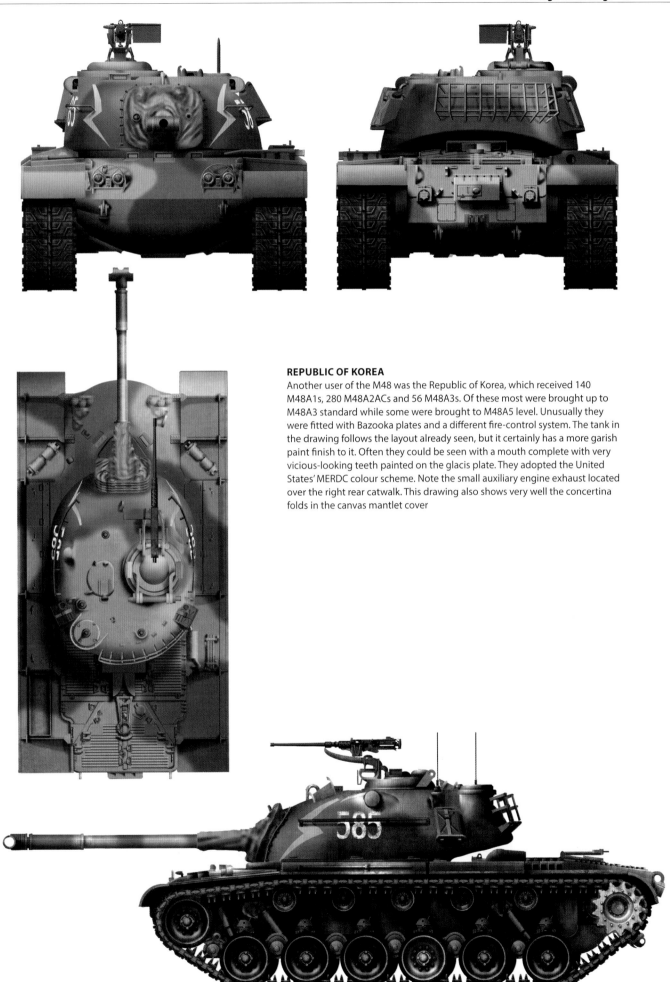

REPUBLIC OF KOREA
Another user of the M48 was the Republic of Korea, which received 140 M48A1s, 280 M48A2ACs and 56 M48A3s. Of these most were brought up to M48A3 standard while some were brought to M48A5 level. Unusually they were fitted with Bazooka plates and a different fire-control system. The tank in the drawing follows the layout already seen, but it certainly has a more garish paint finish to it. Often they could be seen with a mouth complete with very vicious-looking teeth painted on the glacis plate. They adopted the United States' MERDC colour scheme. Note the small auxiliary engine exhaust located over the right rear catwalk. This drawing also shows very well the concertina folds in the canvas mantlet cover

M48A3-VN

This shows a United States Marine Corps M48A3 fitted with the Continental AVDS 1970 diesel engine. This was a major step forward and created a different rear part of the tank. Due to the fitting of the double-louvered doors at the rear, some fittings had to be relocated: the tank telephone was moved to the right rear catwalk. The tank is fitted with the licence-built British L7 105mm tank gun, which for quite a long time was the standard gun for NATO. Even the early M1 Abrams were fitted with it. Very hard to pick out on a drawing but the one feature of this gun was the fact that the fume extractor was not fitted concentrically as all other guns were. It was mounted eccentrically, thus looking at it head-on it will look as if it has slipped to one side. The reason for this was to prevent damage when using stabilizers on the Centurion to stop it banging hard on the rear deck. The commander has also got the M1 cupola but it is fitted with the riser to give him more all-round vision. Mounted on the mantlet is a Zenon searchlight which is in a rather precarious location. It would not be until M48A5 that a storage box for the light when not in use was introduced. The paint scheme is finished in all-over United States Marine Corps green.

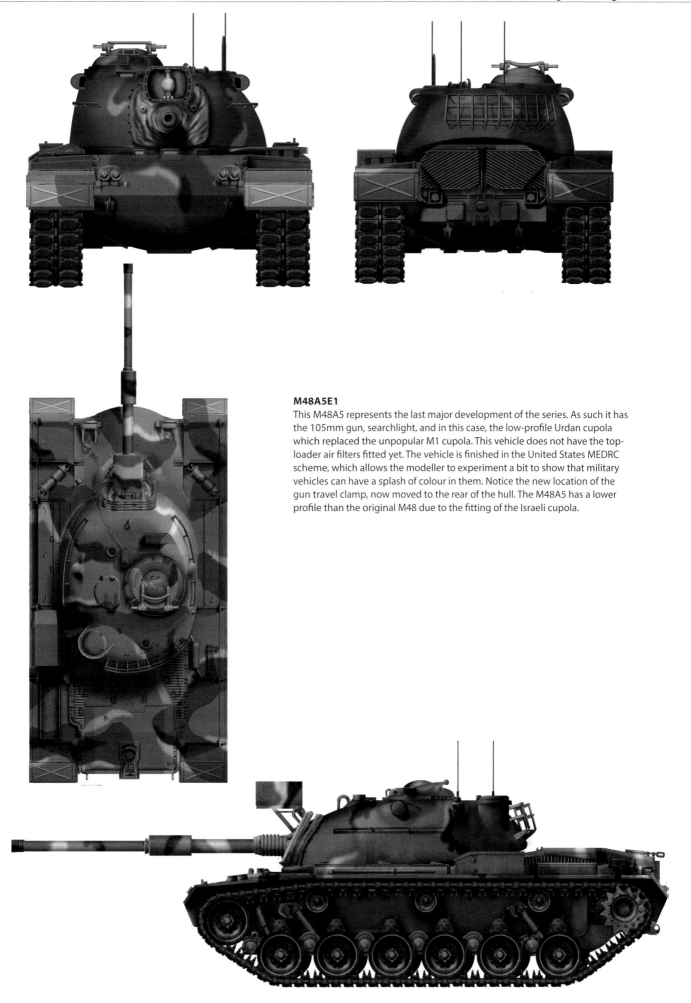

M48A5E1

This M48A5 represents the last major development of the series. As such it has the 105mm gun, searchlight, and in this case, the low-profile Urdan cupola which replaced the unpopular M1 cupola. This vehicle does not have the top-loader air filters fitted yet. The vehicle is finished in the United States MEDRC scheme, which allows the modeller to experiment a bit to show that military vehicles can have a splash of colour in them. Notice the new location of the gun travel clamp, now moved to the rear of the hull. The M48A5 has a lower profile than the original M48 due to the fitting of the Israeli cupola.

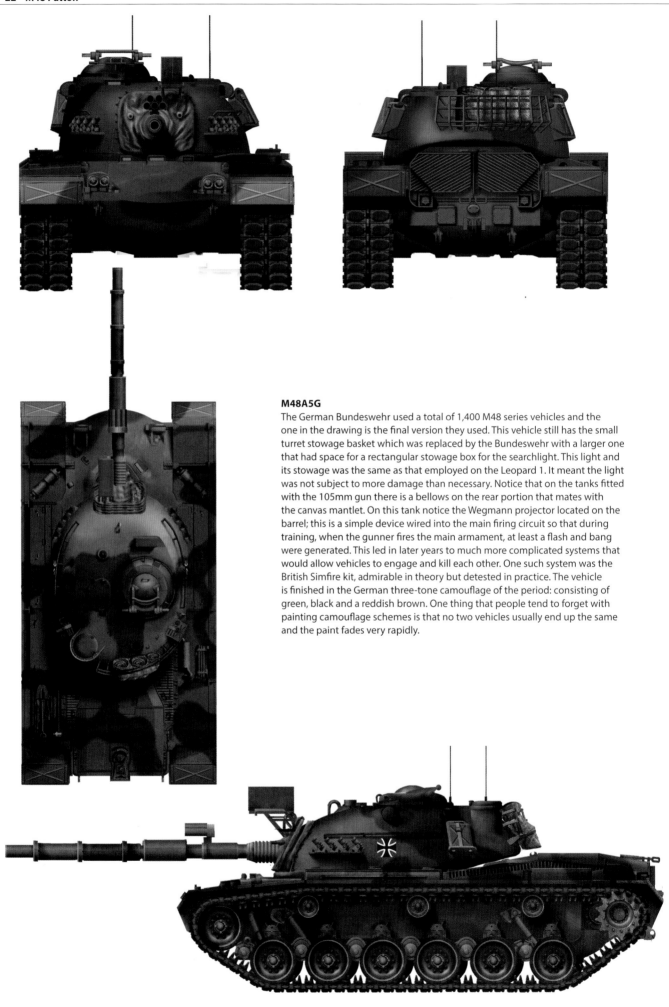

M48A5G

The German Bundeswehr used a total of 1,400 M48 series vehicles and the one in the drawing is the final version they used. This vehicle still has the small turret stowage basket which was replaced by the Bundeswehr with a larger one that had space for a rectangular stowage box for the searchlight. This light and its stowage was the same as that employed on the Leopard 1. It meant the light was not subject to more damage than necessary. Notice that on the tanks fitted with the 105mm gun there is a bellows on the rear portion that mates with the canvas mantlet. On this tank notice the Wegmann projector located on the barrel; this is a simple device wired into the main firing circuit so that during training, when the gunner fires the main armament, at least a flash and bang were generated. This led in later years to much more complicated systems that would allow vehicles to engage and kill each other. One such system was the British Simfire kit, admirable in theory but detested in practice. The vehicle is finished in the German three-tone camouflage of the period: consisting of green, black and a reddish brown. One thing that people tend to forget with painting camouflage schemes is that no two vehicles usually end up the same and the paint fades very rapidly.

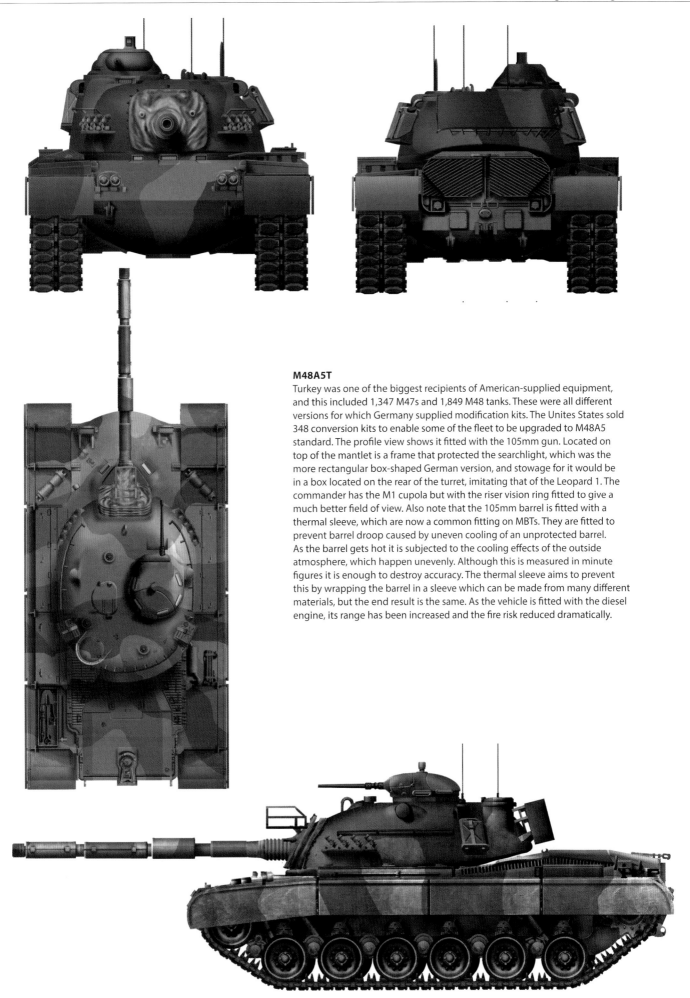

M48A5T

Turkey was one of the biggest recipients of American-supplied equipment, and this included 1,347 M47s and 1,849 M48 tanks. These were all different versions for which Germany supplied modification kits. The Unites States sold 348 conversion kits to enable some of the fleet to be upgraded to M48A5 standard. The profile view shows it fitted with the 105mm gun. Located on top of the mantlet is a frame that protected the searchlight, which was the more rectangular box-shaped German version, and stowage for it would be in a box located on the rear of the turret, imitating that of the Leopard 1. The commander has the M1 cupola but with the riser vision ring fitted to give a much better field of view. Also note that the 105mm barrel is fitted with a thermal sleeve, which are now a common fitting on MBTs. They are fitted to prevent barrel droop caused by uneven cooling of an unprotected barrel. As the barrel gets hot it is subjected to the cooling effects of the outside atmosphere, which happen unevenly. Although this is measured in minute figures it is enough to destroy accuracy. The thermal sleeve aims to prevent this by wrapping the barrel in a sleeve which can be made from many different materials, but the end result is the same. As the vehicle is fitted with the diesel engine, its range has been increased and the fire risk reduced dramatically.

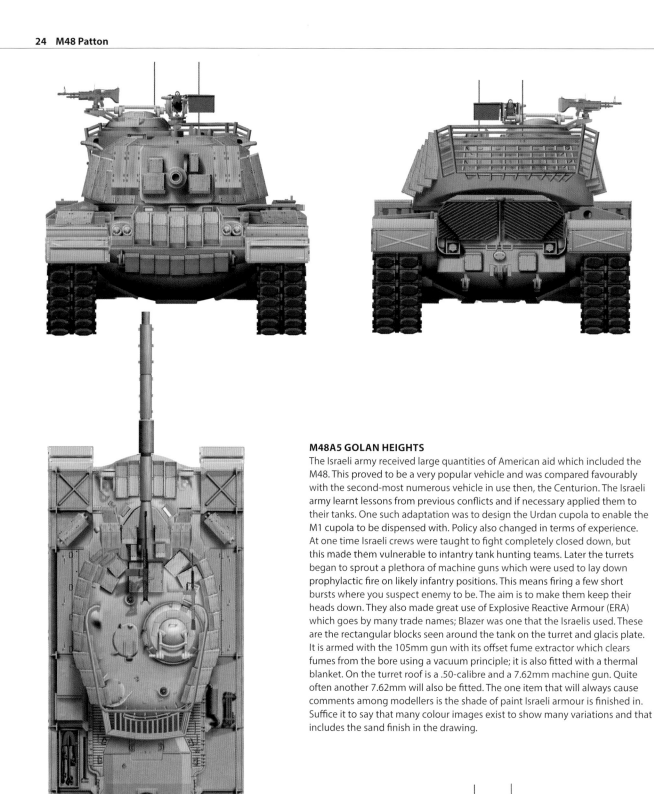

M48A5 GOLAN HEIGHTS

The Israeli army received large quantities of American aid which included the M48. This proved to be a very popular vehicle and was compared favourably with the second-most numerous vehicle in use then, the Centurion. The Israeli army learnt lessons from previous conflicts and if necessary applied them to their tanks. One such adaptation was to design the Urdan cupola to enable the M1 cupola to be dispensed with. Policy also changed in terms of experience. At one time Israeli crews were taught to fight completely closed down, but this made them vulnerable to infantry tank hunting teams. Later the turrets began to sprout a plethora of machine guns which were used to lay down prophylactic fire on likely infantry positions. This means firing a few short bursts where you suspect enemy to be. The aim is to make them keep their heads down. They also made great use of Explosive Reactive Armour (ERA) which goes by many trade names; Blazer was one that the Israelis used. These are the rectangular blocks seen around the tank on the turret and glacis plate. It is armed with the 105mm gun with its offset fume extractor which clears fumes from the bore using a vacuum principle; it is also fitted with a thermal blanket. On the turret roof is a .50-calibre and a 7.62mm machine gun. Quite often another 7.62mm will also be fitted. The one item that will always cause comments among modellers is the shade of paint Israeli armour is finished in. Suffice it to say that many colour images exist to show many variations and that includes the sand finish in the drawing.

PATTON M48A3

2nd Battalion, 34th Armoured Regiment, Vietnam 1969–1970

1/35 scale

Anthony Leone

The 2nd Battalion, 34th Armoured Regiment (known as the Dreadnaughts) took part in operations supporting the 25th Infantry Division in Vietnam 1969–1970. Images of the 2/34 tanks are few and so grainy that many details are lost. However, it's clear that some of the 2/34 tanks supporting the 25th Infantry featured field-mounted M60 machine guns, and the distinctive shields seen on M113s in front of the loader's hatch. These vehicles also saw the .50-calibre machine gun field-mounted to the outside of the commander's cupola, a common practice among Patton crews during Vietnam. The base kit is the Dragon M48A3. This particular kit comes supplied with a mantlet with moulded cover and the iconic Xenon searchlight (the M48A3 Mod B kit from Dragon does not come with these features). In general the base kit builds up well and the level of detail is very good, but I found the key features that enticed me to seek out this kit ultimately needed updating.

While the kit-supplied mantlet with cover and Xenon searchlight assembly initially felt like a bonus, there were issues of scale and fidelity in these features. As the searchlight is such a focal point and I was intent on including one on this tank, I purchased the Legend M48A3 Mantlet kit that comes with both a well-moulded searchlight and detailed mantlet and cover.

The Dragon kit comes with well-printed decals for five different tanks. However, I was unsure of the accuracy of the graphics, so decided not to use the kit decals. I kept things simple and used dry transfer stars that I had on hand.

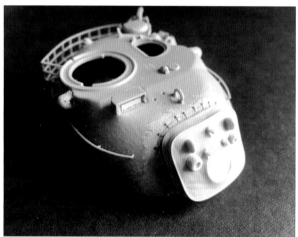

The Legend Mantlet kit consists of a large two-piece resin assembly that requires a good-sized mounting hole to be drilled and cut in the front of the turret. This took some delicacy, especially as I was undertaking this procedure after much of the turret was already assembled.

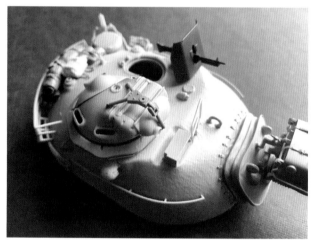

The M60 mounts on the Tamiya M113 Armored Cavalry kit gave me the idea to build a 2/34 Patton. I was loaned an M60 mount from a M113 kit on the condition that I make it removable. I try to find one element to make a model interesting or unique and this was it.

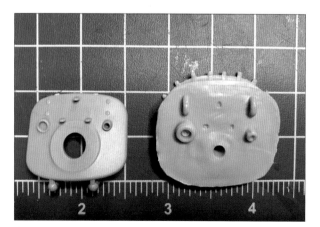

The kit-supplied mantlet with moulded cover (right) looks a little like a pancake and is a bit oversized compared with the mantlet without the cover (left).

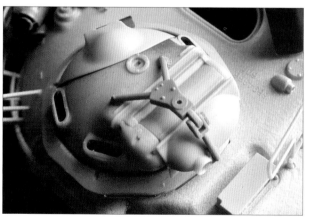

One of the finer features of the kit is the commander's cupola and riser. The vision ports in the cupola are moulded in clear plastic and form a separate mould attached to the base ring.

Notably, registration numbers are missing from this build. The registration decals provided in the kit are of individual numbers, which are a real challenge to align during application. As I didn't find many images with clear registration-number references for this unit, I opted to leave them off entirely.

The kit comes supplied with Dragon DS tracks. While these are moulded very well, the fit is a little loose which makes it challenging for the tracks to lie naturally on the upper return rollers. Anyone wishing to use the kit tracks can probably remove a link to achieve a tighter fit. I opted for a set of AFV Club tracks.

The model was crowned with the excellent .50-calibre machine gun from Tasca, but the modern ammo bin and mount is from the Academy machine-gun set. For a better field of fire, Patton crews field-mounted the .50-cals to the outside of the turret by welding a modified tripod to the cupola.

During my research I came across an image of a Vietnam-era M48A3 with a large peace sign drawn on the front of the Xenon light cover. I thought it would be interesting to contrast this symbol against the up-gunned 2/34 version, festooned with ammo bins and gear. My only gripe about the Legend kit is the sagging light cover.

The turret basket was overfilled with stowage and gear. Notably some nice pieces from Value Gear as well as some handmade tarps to fill out the baskets. The build was topped off with a couple of soda and beer cans from a Tamiya M113 kit.

Many Vietnam-era Pattons were loaded with spare ammo bins. The .50-calibre, .30-calibre, and 40mm bins are from the AFV Club Cal.30/Cal.50/40mm Modern US Ammunition Box set. A few well-detailed boxes from the Academy Machine Gun set are dotted about as well. The ammo bins are painted in shades of olive drab.

The handles on the searchlight are made from brass rod that was supplied with the Legend kit. These took some care and are rather delicate – they broke twice during the remainder of assembly. I added the strap details (made of candy wrapper foil) to support the cover on the back of the light, as these are not provided in the Legend Mantlet kit.

The Dragon kit finishes as an excellent rendition of a Vietnam-era M48A3 Patton, despite the frustration of having to update the mantlet and searchlight. Once the final model was loaded up with stowage, and given a good coating of dust and dirt, I dare say I was inspired to build another one.

I mixed Tamiya olive drab and dark green for the base coat and lightened it on the upper surfaces with dark yellow. The subsequent weathering and pigment phases strongly influence the final appearance anyway.

Spare AFV Track links were hung from the turret handrails. I had to drill out little holes in the upper guide teeth to properly connect the tracks to the handrails.

PATTON M48A2C
Tet Offensive, Vietnam 1968
1/35 scale
David Nickles

This is the old 1/35 Monogram kit which dates back to 1958. For an old kit, it is still fundamentally accurate overall. When I built this model, the newer kits from Dragon and Revell were not available, and only the old Tamiya M48A3 kit and its Academy cousin were available to work with. I like to build these old models and update them to modern standards, while still using as much of the original kit as possible. I feel that just replacing everything doesn't show what you can do with the old kit, because, in the end, so little of it will be left. This M48 represents a generic M48A2C sent to Vietnam as a replacement to make up for losses incurred during the 1968 Tet Offensive. The M48A3 was the main vehicle used in Vietnam, but some A2C versions were sent after Tet. Monogram's kit actually represents the M48A2. The main external difference between the types is that the A2C lacks the track tensioning idler wheel, so this was simply omitted from the kit. I used the Vietnam decals provided with the kit, going along with my intention to use as much of what came with the model as possible, so I make no claims as to their accuracy.

The lower hull was built essentially out of the box, except the track tensioning idler was deleted.

Some minor detailing was done to the headlight brackets.

The commander's cupola had the .50-calibre barrel removed and a complete M2 .50 added on top, as was common in Vietnam. A 7.62mm M60 machine gun was added to the loader's position with a scratch-built mount and shield. The gun came from the old Tamiya Armoured Infantry set.

I used the kit decals and deliberately inverted the peace sign which was done in the 1960s and 1970s as a symbol of anti-war protest. Painting was simple enough: the whole model was primed with Tamiya aerosol JGSDF olive drab lacquer, which is a perfect match for US Vietnam-era dark olive drab. Then, the model was highlighted using an airbrush and the jar version of JGSDF olive, lightened with yellow green.

Details like the mantlet cover, guns, spare tracks and stowage were all picked out in various Vallejo acrylic paints. Weathering was simply some dark enamel washes and both loose and airbrushed Mig pigments. To airbrush the pigments mix a bit in with well-thinned clear flat and spray it onto the model for a dust effect.

The Patton's turret received the most work. The moulded-on hand rails were sanded off and replaced by new ones made from plastic rod. Likewise, the kit's rear stowage bin brackets were thinned down, and all the bracing was made from plastic rod as well. The stereoscopic gun sight apertures were opened up with a drill, as was the muzzle brake.

I did have a set of spare Tamiya M48 tracks and those were used to replace the chunky kit tracks. The Tamiya tracks fit perfectly and made a noticeable difference.

Some basic stowage was added to the rear bustle using some homemade tarps and rolls and Vietnam-era spare parts.

A gun mantlet cover was made by cutting some plastic baffles, shaped like the mantlet shield, and gluing them in place behind the mantlet. Then, the mantlet and baffles were blended in using Vallejo acrylic putty. Epoxy putty would have been better. The acrylic putty did the job with several applications.

The kit's clunky front mud flaps were cut away and the exposed edges thinned a bit. The engineering of the kit makes it difficult to do a lot here without totally reworking everything.

PATTON M48A3
C Company, 69th Armoured Regiment USMC, Vietnam 1968
1/35 scale
Ben Skipper

Deciding on which version of the iconic M48 to build can be a bit of a challenge. I went straight to Tamiya as it is familiar ground choosing their venerable M48A3 (#35120*2500 MM120) kit. Well designed, this kit really did fall together with parts being removed and added without complaint. I chose to model a US Army Vietnam-era M48A3. This gave me the opportunity to add some unique detailing, using resin equipment add-ons from Panzer Art, Legend and Black Dog and photoetch from Eduard. Overall a great little kit which lends itself to being a brilliant build either out of the box or, with a little patience, a platform ripe for some radical modification.

Preparing the turret for the Legend gun mantle cover. A lot of checking and double checking here. The Legend resin mantlet is held in place with Milliput filler and sellotape whilst position is finalized before being epoxyed into place. The Legend mantlet is blended into the turret with Milliput using a wet painter pallet knife. The Milliput filler around the new resin mantle has been left to dry for 48 hours. A quick rub down around the mantlet with 1500 grit wet & dry helps to form and blend the filler in with the turret surrounds. This is then covered with Mr Surfacer 1000.

The first task was to change the kit's gun mount for Legend's beautifully cast resin shroud and lamp (the lamp would not be used). After some cutting, filling and sanding, the mount was in place and the turret halves joined. The turret is topped with the commander's cupola. A little bit of work really brings it to life. This picture shows the test fit of the commander's cupola with its unique riser, and a final squaring away of filling around the resin mantlet.

Bronco workable track link set (T97E2) made from brown-coloured traditional plastic, features nearly 1,000 parts. I used a piece of straight-sided metal to help keep things in check. Revell's precision cement applicator was a boon for this task. The kit road wheels were replaced with Panzer Art resin road wheels as they have the detailing on the rear. Well cast with little flash, they added a realistic touch and welcome weight. Here the road wheels have been glued and are curing well.

Mating the two hull halves together is relatively straightforward. A small poly cap helps align the front while the rear sits on the engine bay access doors. Here the resultant seam from joining the hull halves has been sanded and covered with Mr Surfacer 1000.

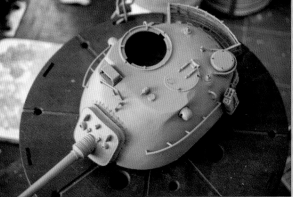

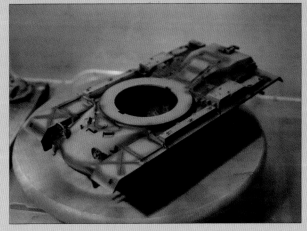

The turret, road wheels and tracks are added to the completed hull, giving the modeller a handsome vehicle. This is the final test fit before priming: note the etched parts around the mantlet that would hold the canvas cover in place and the detailing etch along the hull sides as well as the handles for the various storage lockers located on the track cover decks. The gun barrel is added at this point, ready for painting. I've left the large searchlight, horn and night driving light off the kit as photos shows they were often removed in theatre.

Primed and ready. The lower and rear hull have been sprayed grey and then matt black, whilst panel line and shadow areas are pre-shaded with a dark green.

Prior to painting I always recommend a primer base coat; it also helps to secure photo-etched parts. The kit's finishing instructions are clear and provide the modeller with several options. In this instance I wanted to go for something a little different so used Star Decals which went on with little problem.

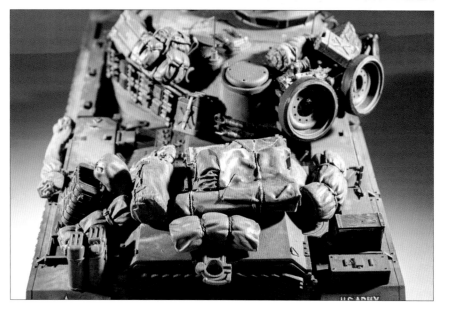

The final task is to load her up and make her ready for a trip into the bush with a range of Black Dog, Legend and Tamiya details such as sacking, body armour and ammo boxes. One little detail I always add is the radio antennas, I use a bristle from a small brush. Once the final stores are loaded, the spare track sections on hung from the turret's side, ammo boxes are secured with wire and antennas are pressed into service to complete the model. Final checks are made and the kit is allowed to settle as the glue dries before the first of weathering coats is added.

First, a mix of ground red pastel, mixed into a paste with white spirit is added, with attention being paid to the wheels and lower hull in particular. Finally, an application of bauxite coloured mud is added, with attention being paid to areas of crew transit and the sides of the track boards. Once dry the excess is removed and the model is left to air and dry.

PATTON M48A3
3rd Tank Battalion, USMC, Vietnam 1965
1/35 scale
Bill Stewart

The Tamiya M48A3 was originally released as a motorized model kit in 1983, one of the last of what I would consider the classic Tamiya kits. The model goes together very well, and for the casual builder will build into a fine M48A3 straight out on the box. However, the kit does have its shortcomings, some of which stem from it being a nearly 40-year-old kit with simplified detail. It also suffers from having an inaccurate stance: the tank sits too high in the rear. I planned to address the running-gear issue, replace the vinyl tracks with an aftermarket set, and refine some of the more chunky details of the model to improve what is basically a sound, classic kit.

The kit is a mid-production M48A3 that features a ring of vision blocks for the commander, sandwiched between the cupola and turret. I decided to build an earlier version by eliminating the vision ring, as well as the large trademark searchlight commonly seen on many Pattons in the field. I wanted to depict a tank that had seen plenty of action, but one that was well cared for by the crew. I chose to remove the front portion of both fenders, indicating that one or both had suffered damage and were subsequently removed by the crew. This was also an opportunity to show off the aggressive tracks and the mud and filth this tank would have churned up in the field.

The majority of the Pattons in wartime photos were packed with tarps, gear, tools, ammo boxes, spare wheels and tracks, and many other items the crew had found. I decided to rebuild the clunky turret stowage basket with a more to-scale selection of styrene rod and strips. The new basket provided the opportunity to load it up with a selection of such items. I took advantage of what was mostly a collection of drab colours to punctuate the stowage with such details as a case of beer, ration cartons and a camouflaged helmet for visual interest.

To obtain the right USMC Vietnam-era olive drab, I used Tamiya XF-74 OD (JGSDF) as a base coat followed by randomly-applied lighter tones of XF-74, lightened with buff to create a haphazardly faded finish. Prior to applying decals I hand-brushed the build with several coats of acrylic floor wax. After the decals had set up, I again coated the hull and turret with acrylic floor wax to seal the paint in preparation for the heavy weathering to come. To replicate the slight sheen on Vietnam-era Pattons, I applied a very light coat of Dullcote to help flatten the finish a bit. Details were painted with various Vallejo colors.

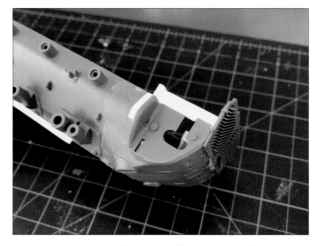

The belly of the hull is plagued by a number of holes from the old days of motorized models. I filled all the holes with sheet styrene and sanded the surface flush. Here I also tacked on a pair of temporary rails, strips of .080" styrene, to the underside of the tubes where the suspension swing arms would be installed. These rails are necessary for the hull levelling procedure.

In the rear of the lower hull, I created additional styrene filler parts for missing sections of the hull walls surrounding where the final drive would be mounted.

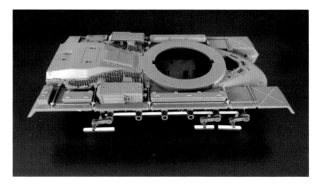

Prior to levelling the suspension, I cemented the upper and lower halves of the hull together. I then checked for warpage of the hull by placing it (with the temporary rails installed) on a flat surface to check for any rocking. I removed the bump stops from the swing arms, being careful to label the now-separate parts. I then mounted each swing arm in place with a .060 styrene spacer under each arm to ensure a level set of axles for the road wheels. This step is critical to correcting the inclined stance of the model. Once the cement had set, I trimmed each bump stop to fit with the repositioned swing arms.

Weathering began with a combination of dark-pin washes and dust/dirt/mud area washes of Winsor Newton oil paints. The lower hull and running gear were treated to several applications of Mig pigments to build up layers of dried and damp mud. Spots of wear in the paint, where the filth had been removed by crew traffic, were highlighted by dry brushing darkened olive drab. Spots where the paint had been worn off were treated to spots of rust wash and graphite for bare metal.

The bump stops are missing a series of fillets that protrude from the sides of the hull. I added fillets of putty pressed into shape with a section of brass rod. I cleaned up the excess putty with an x-acto, and coated the entire lower hull with Mr. Surfacer to simulate a cast texture. This detail will be covered with mud and largely obscured by the large road wheels.

To guarantee a tight fit with the aftermarket tracks, it is necessary to modify the mounting of the idler wheel so that it can swing forward to take up any excess slack in the tracks. I drilled a hole where the mounting pin was, and fastened the swing arm to the hull with a tiny flat head screw.

The tracks were assembled in straight flat sections for the top and bottom runs with Tamiya Extra Thin cement brushed on to make the assemblies permanent. The remaining sections that wrap around the front idler and drive sprocket were left workable until a final fitting. The sprue section appearing to stick out of the drive sprocket is a tool I made from a single-end connector glued to a scrap of sprue to hold the track together during test fitting. I used this tool until the tracks were installed for good, with a final-end connector cemented in place.

Once the assembled tracks had been fitted, I pushed the idler arm forward to a snug position and brushed on a bit of Tamiya Extra Thin cement to permanently secure the idler arm in place. At this time I also brushed the same thin cement onto the end connectors of each track link to set their form, being careful not to accidentally glue the tracks to the road wheels. After the cement had cured and the tracks were stiff they were removed for painting and detailing.

The fit of the turret is somewhat sloppy, with a substantial overhang around the turret perimeter. Using the turret race on the hull as a reference and a circle template as a guide, I carefully filed and sanded the turret walls to match the shape of the hull's form. Removing this much material leaves the turret wall pretty thin, so I strengthened the inside front of the turret with Apoxie Sculpt putty first.

I decided to scratch build and sculpt a new mantlet cover out of Apoxie Sculpt putty, a styrene rod and numerous lead strips for mounting clips. In this picture you can see the sheen of the newly applied cast texture created by stippling Testors Liquid (black bottle) cement onto the turret surface with an old stiff paintbrush.

The kit barrel was moulded in two halves, and in most cases I would replace it with an aftermarket brass or aluminum barrel, but with some careful cleanup I was able to get the barrel looking right. The muzzle brake is not moulded correctly – the actual brake has a stepped seam where it meets the barrel – but I was able to detail the kit version to an acceptable place by thinning the edges with an x-acto and a round file.

Many of the M48s in photos from Vietnam show severely damaged or missing front fenders. I elected to remove the forward sections of both front fenders, imagining that the crew had taken them off after suffering damage in the field. I thinned the remaining styrene and added tiny holes where the bolts from the missing portions would have been mounted.

It is fair to say that for an armoured fighting vehicle with a fair amount of battle honours to its credit, the M48 Patton does appear to be the poor relation when it comes to suitable model kits. In 1958, some five years after the tank was first purchased by the US Army, **Monogram** released their first 1/35 model kit of the M48A2. This kit was to be re-boxed on no less than five occasions, the last being 2011, and is still available today. The initial Monogram box art featured an action-filled scene that would have more than appealed to the modeller of the time: a modeller living in a world of brightly illustrated action superhero comics and adventures. Colour highlighted wording combined dynamically with imposing fat-face fonts. The contrasting *exclusive features* element, combined with the wonderfully painted battle scene, featuring the M48 working with dismounted infantry, made for an eye-catching purchase. The kit itself was moulded in olive drab plastic, except for the black vinyl

tracks. Even now it is worth noting the sharpness of the casting, in particular of the road wheels. The barrel itself comes as a single-piece moulding, which needs a little bit of attention to give it an authentic appearance. The instructions are clearly presented in booklet form and easy to interpret. The hull itself is split into four parts, with the lower hull being split down the centre, this is then capped with the lower part of the upper hull which features the return rollers. On top of this sits the upper hull with its moulded engine deck and track covers, which feature some wonderful details, including a shovel and pickaxe, all of which are well executed. The turret, with its unique ballistic curves, is well defined and is attached to the upper hull with a single stub pin. This model can still be found on a host of internet sites under the Revell brand number 85-7853.

(This section is written and compiled by Ben Skipper)

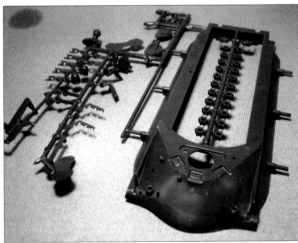

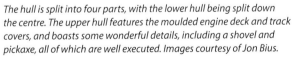

The hull is split into four parts, with the lower hull being split down the centre. The upper hull features the moulded engine deck and track covers, and boasts some wonderful details, including a shovel and pickaxe, all of which are well executed. Images courtesy of Jon Bius.

In its long history the Monogram M48A2 1/35 scale kit has been re-boxed many times. Each time the box art is indicative of the decade it is released into. What are garish colours today were the norm in the 1950s. Images courtesy of Jon Bius.

The casting is sharp and the moulding detailed. The instructions are clearly presented and easy to interpret. The kit comes with six dismounted infantrymen and a tank commander and driver (half). Tracks and sprockets are usually the first item to be replaced on this aging kit. AFV Club makes a set of tracks for the M48/60/88 series of vehicles. Many modellers use these to update the current kits. Images courtesy of Jon Bius.

Images courtesy of Creative Models.

In 1964 **Tamiya** entered the fray with their 1/35 popular production of the M48. The first production was the A2 (without searchlight) followed in 1983 by the A3 version (MM120). The box art really spoils the modeller, with Tamiya wheeling out Shigeru Komatsuzaki's wonderful rendition of a Vietnam-era US Marine Corps M48A3. On the box's side panels are the alternative Shark Mouth finish and an interesting visual juxtaposition between the M48 and the subsequent US tank model to bear the Patton name, the M60. This kit is widely acknowledged as the go-to kit for modellers of the M48. As with anything Tamiya this kit practically builds itself, but there is a key feature to note: it was initially designed to hold an electric motor. As such there are a few unfortunate gaps and apertures, although thankfully these are placed out of sight and do not detract from the model itself. It is moulded in olive drab plastic; the sprues being reasonably clean in appearance. There are noticeable mould lines on most parts, but given the age of the kit and that it is injection moulded, as opposed to slide moulded, this is hardly surprising and doesn't detract from the overall finish. Detail does on occasion appear at the wrong places,

but can be addressed with prudent sanding and weathering. The vinyl tracks are delightfully detailed, supplied in Tamiya's special metallic black finish. As the tracks are thick enough, a length holds itself together with little persuasion, eschewing the need for additional strengthening with thread or staples. Decals are made in-house and are of the usual Tamiya clarity, the yellow is well within register with no bleed on the overlaying colours or shades. The kit is a relatively straightforward build, with the instructions printed out clearly. It consists of a two-piece hull built from the ground up. The turret rendition is sharp and once the two halves are together it really presents a handsome model ripe for either a clean display or can be stacked high with goodies for diorama use. The rear deck plating is spot on, with Tamiya's engineers taking note of subtleties in the prototype's appearance and ensuring these are incorporated into the finished model, especially the engine's rear-panel details. Overall this really is a reasonably priced kit suitable for any modeller wishing to dabble in an icon of American armour and is arguably the most accessible of the 1/35 scale offerings.

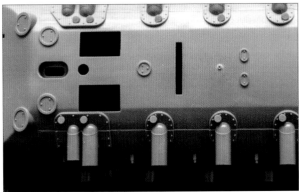

As this is an old, injection-moulded kit there are noticeable mould lines.

The turret rendition is sharp.

Due to the old electric motor there are gaps and apertures that will need filling.

When the turret and hull are joined it really presents a handsome model ripe for display.

The upper and lower hull have been fitted together and the resultant seam sanded and covered with Mr Surfacer 1000.

The vinyl tracks are detailed and supplied in their metallic black finish although some modellers prefer to replace them. Images courtesy of Tamiya and internationalscalemodeler.com

Takom have really pushed the boat out with their 2017 offering of the M48-H/CM-11, Brave Tiger MBT (Takom 2090). This variant of the M48 was developed between General Dynamics and the Republic of China Army (ROCA) Armoured Vehicle Development Centre. The kit's box art, by Jason, is beautifully executed and shows how the M48 design, nearly 70 years old, is still a formidable-looking armoured vehicle. The action setting, allied with the three-tone camouflage, make for one of the more eye-catching contemporary representations of the M48. Supplied with a range of plastic, vinyl, photo-etch and metal parts, Takom has really gone all out to present the modeller not only with a challenge, but a reasonably-priced model of the latest incarnation of this iconic Cold War warrior. The grey plastic sprues are well engineered and the moulding is sharp, with the bare minimum of mould lines present. Many of the detailing elements, such as locker handles have been moulded as separate elements, thus adding body to the build. Of particular interest is the manner in which the running gear is assembled. Here Takom has really taken the time to look at the details of the suspension assembly which differs from earlier M48

variants and has more in common with the M60. A nice touch is the road wheel build sequence, which features separate road tyres for the outer facing wheels. The vinyl tracks are of the later pattern and of a decent thickness, that, like the Tamiya offering, are sturdy enough. Interestingly, instead of relying on heat, staples, thread or glue they are joined together by fine metal pins. The bonus here is that the track remains flexible at the join, therefore being more lifelike and lacking that dreaded flat section of traditional joins that other kits often suffer from. Decals, few as they are, are supplied as either hi-colour, non-tactical and subdued-tactical markings. These are from Takom and seem to be clear and in register with no bleeding. The small sheet of photo-etch, supplied for lining the basket bushel, is well engineered and cleanly cut into the sheet. The 20-step instructions – although featuring the Explosive Reactive Armour appliqué armoured variant on the cover, which isn't covered by this particular edition – are presented as a booklet and are clear throughout. It concludes with a detailed painting plan that allows the modeller to faithfully reproduce the ROCA combat finish.

Contemporary box art promises a well-engineered kit with sharp moulding and the Takom kit does not disappoint.

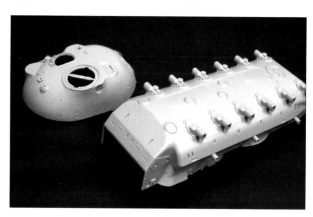

A miminum of mould lines are present on this modern kit. Image courtesy of luckymodel.com

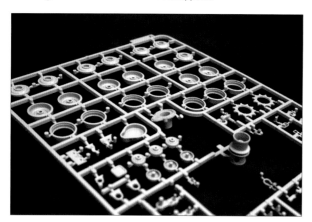

The road wheel build sequence features separate road tyres for the outer facing wheels. Image courtesy of luckymodel.com

The vinyl tracks are of the later pattern and of a decent thickness. Image courtesy of luckymodel.com

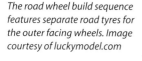

Takom's CM11 or M48H profile has all of the classic M48 DNA but with a more contemporary finish. The M68 main gun, remodeled commander's cupola and updated imaging and range-finding equipment. Of note is the M239 smoke grenade launcher sited on both sides of the turret behind the gun mantlet. Image courtesy of Aaron Skinner finescaler.com

The final manufacturer of M48 kits worth mentioning is **Dragon**. For years Dragon has produced some simply stunning kits, being the leader in multi-media models that contain everything for the modeller to create a miniature masterpiece. While one could continue to wax lyrical about Dragon, their kits aren't for beginners. The instructions, while always well printed, are often 'busy' and challenge most builders' concentration. The M48A1 version combines some aspects of the M46 and M47 that armour enthusiast will recognize: including the Tension Compensating Idler Wheel, the curved front and rear fenders, as well as the lower commander's cupola, all of which have been accurately recreated in Dragon's 2016 issue of the kit. What makes this kit stand out is the use of the in-house DS material for the tracks and gun mantel cover. The caramel-coloured Dragon Styrene 100 (DS), was developed specifically by Dragon's in-house research and development team and is a unique plastic that combines the best aspects of polystyrene and vinyl. Delicate details can be reproduced with DS using both under-cut and slide

moulding, reducing the number of small parts. Another boon is that DS parts can be cemented with ordinary plastic cement. The kit is presented with an interesting cover painting by the renowned artist Auletta. The rear of the tank has been illustrated, presumably to show off its difference from subsequent M48s. The tank has been placed in a desert setting, which could easily place it as an M48 deployed in Lebanon during the summer and autumn of 1958. Indeed, Dragon has included decals for such a vehicle as well as an M48 in use with the Bundeswehr.Moulded in grey plastic, the kit is atypical of Dragon offerings in that it is a mix of old kit and new tooled sprues, and gifts the modeller with a raft of spares for future projects. The hull and turret are subtly textured, with the hull appearing to have been slide moulded while the remainder of the kit has been injection moulded. The etched parts are minimal, yet add important details to the kit. A length of wire is supplied for the recovery tow ropes. The decal sheet, while not expansive is produced in-house and is sharp in definition with no colour bleed.

The M48A1 version combines some aspects of the M46 and M47 that armour enthusiasts will recognize: including the Tension Compensating Idler Wheel, the curved front and rear fenders, as well as the lower commander cupola. Images courtesy of Gino P. Quintiliani.

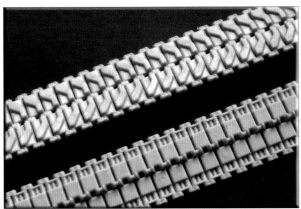

What makes this kit stand out is the use of the in-house DS material for the tracks and gun mantel cover. Images courtesy of Gino P. Quintiliani.

Moulded in grey plastic the kit is atypical of Dragon offerings in that it is a mix of old kit and new tooled sprues, and gifts the modeller with a raft of spares for future projects. Images courtesy of Gino P. Quintiliani.

While the M48 tank model kit list isn't extensive there are a great deal of second-hand offerings from Revell, AFV Club, Academy, ERTL and Italeri, and new products from favoured manufacturers are on the horizon. There are also numerous bid-site offerings of the M48 with some truly amazing versions, including Monogram's 1/48 glow-in-the-dark kit: Luminators Patton Tank, part of its Neon Warriors range, kit Nr. 1615.

Current Model Kits of M48:

- AFV Club HF018, 1/35 M48 AVLB Bridge Layer
- AFV Club/ Hobby Fan HF018, 1/35 M48 AVLB, resin model kit
- Dragon D3559, 1/35 M48A1
- Dragon D3544, 1/35 M48A3. Mod B
- Dragon D3546, 1/35 M48A3
- Dragon D3611, 1/35 M48A5 105mm Gun
- Dragon D3606, 1/35 M48 AVLB Bridge Layer
- Revell Nr. 85-7853, 1/35 M48A2

- Revell Nr. 03206, 1/35 M48A2/A2C
- Revell Nr. 03236, 1/35 M48A2GA2
- Takom Nr. 2090, 1/35 M48H/CM11 Brave Tiger
- Tamiya 300035120 (MM120), 1/35 M48A3

Despite the lack of models and their availability, there is a great selection of aftermarket products available to supplement the above-mentioned kits. From a resin IDF Magach 3 with Blazer armour conversion set by Legend to workable track links by Bronco and metal barrels by Orange Hobby, there is something for the most demanding and ambitious modellers.

Aftermarket kit manufacturers
As with all things modelling there are numerous extras that offer additional detailing for kits including decals. To list all their products would be a challenge so details have been split into separate modelling areas and given a brief overview of each manufacturer's output. Some of these detailing kits are examined more closely in the M48A3 build section.

Before starting any major modelling project involving etch it's always best to decide what parts you're going to use and where they fit into the build. This is the Tamiya kit with Eduard etch.

Eduard photo-etch parts. Images courtesy Hannets Models.

Turret bushel liner test fit to the Tamiya kit. The Eduard etch can be attached with liquid poly as the plastic will melt over the etch welding it securely into place.

Generic Fittings and Fixtures

- AGV Models. 1/35 resin gun mantel details
- AFV Club. 1/35 plastic and resin details including tracks and engine
- Barrel Dept. 1/35 turned metal gun barrels
- Black Dog. 1/35 resin accessories including sandbag turret protection as well as personal loads and GI equipment
- Bronco. 1/35 plastic workable tracks
- Def.Model. 1/35 resin and photoetch details including tracks and mantels
- Division Miniature. 1/35 turned metal gun barrels
- Eduard. 1/35 photo-etch detailing sets
- FC Modeltips. 1/35 3D printed accessories
- Friulmodel. 1/35 metal tank tracks
- Legend Productions. 1/35 resin and brass accessories including engine bay
- MR ModellBrau. 1/35 resin details
- Orange Hobby. 1/35 turned metal gun barrels
- Panzerart. 1/35 resin details
- Voyage Models. 1/35 turned metal gun barrels, resin and photo-etch details
- OKB Grigorov. 1/72 plastic and resin details

Vietnam Era

- Black Dog. 1/35 resin accessories including personal loads and GI equipment
- FC Modeltips. 1/35 3D printed accessories
- Legend Productions. 1/35 resin and brass accessories
- Panzerart. 1/35 resin details

IDF Examples

- Accurate Armour. 1/35 resin and photoetch
- Def.Model. 1/35 resin and photo-etch details
- Legend Productions. 1/35 resin and brass accessories

Conversion Kits

- AFV Club/Hobby Fan. 1/35 resin conversion kits
- Bold Division. Resin. 1/35 T110E3 Tankhunter
- Def.Model. 1/35 resin and photo-etch IDF Magach 3 105mm gun
- Legend Productions. 1/35 resin and brass accessories for a range of IDF AFVs
- Perfect Scale Modellbau. 1/35 resin and photoetch A2CG Pioneer Panzer conversion kit
- Modell Trans Modellbau 1/72 resin conversion kits

Decals

- FC Modeltips. 1/35 Spanish Army Service
- LM Decals. 1/35 Hellenic and Cypriot service
- MEC Decals. 1/35 US Army Vietnam/Cold War
- Star Decals. 1/35 US Army, USMC Vietnam

This list is contemporaneous and is subject to change. One important supplier of detailing kits: resin and metal based, but not included due to closure in 2016, is Francois Verlinden. Verlinden is synonymous with quality kits. Sadly these amazing editions are becoming increasingly rare, but worth seeking out nonetheless, especially if you're planning a diorama for your M48.

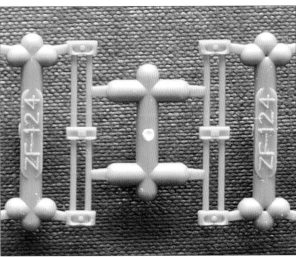

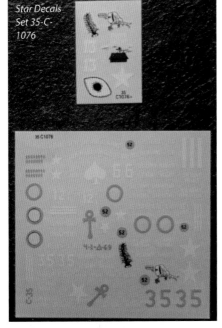

Bronco workable track link set (T97E2). Made from brown-coloured traditional plastic, and featuring near 1,000 parts.

Orange Hobby 90mm M41 Barrel for M48A3 G35-131-80

Left: Legend really knocked the ball out of the park with their beautifully detailed multi-media accessories and modifications sets across a range of genres, none more so than the impressive M48A2GA2 (LF1125/1125-1) multi-media conversion kit for Tamiya's venerable M48A3. It does away with the upper hull, turret and gun set in its entirety and treats the modeller to an exquisitely sculpted cast resin set of replacements.

Below left: Legend's IDF Magach 3 w/Blazer Armour Conversion set for the Tamiya M48A3 kit (LF1134). Here most of the goodies are focused on the turret, replacing the Tamiya kit's version in its entirety. The Israeli Blazer ERA is well finished and without warp, sitting squarely on station.

Below right: The Legend Vietnam special set (LF7204) provides the modeller with what is essentially a diorama in a box. As with all Legend's resin the casting is sharp and the detailing, especially on the wooden ammunition crates, is well defined. This set is for the Tamiya kit and includes a nicely detailed searchlight to replace the kit item.

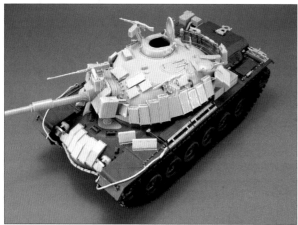

Black Dog are industry leaders of aftermarket resin, their 2013 Modellfan award establishing this. Producing several Vietnam-themed sets, their Big Accessories set for the M48A3 really is a work of art. Delicately cast Bergan frames complete with a whole new rear bustle section that is crammed with food containers, helmets, entrenching tools and partially covered with a tarpaulin. The mass of sandbags have been moulded to ensure they conform to the shape of the turret. Many have been modelled to appear realistically flat and lifelike insofar as the contents would have settled over time and been further compacted by the monsoon rains. Held in place by their own weight, the sandbags are supported by extra track sections protruding from the hull sides. Ammunition boxes, in several sizes, are well cast and are supported by well-designed jerry cans. A particularly nice touch is a spare flak jacket. While this kit is designed primarily for Dragon's M48 with a little work this set will fit nicely on the Tamiya M48. It's fair to say that Black Dog really has delivered an absolute master class in both modelling and observation.

When modelling the M48 there really is a wonderful diversity of variants to choose from. This model from Brian Richardson show just what can be achieved with research, plasticard and bits and pieces from the spares box.

Above: A view across the turret. Note the masking tape over the gunner's sight head. This is probably to protect it when the vehicle was last sprayed. Also a good view of the top of the stowage bins. (Erik Torp Prime Portal)

Left: Looking onto the commander's cupola we can just make out how the commander's machine-gun mount is fitted to the cupola and the fittings on it to receive the actual machine gun. Notice that the periscopes are not fitted and the spring-loaded flaps are in the closed position. (Erik Torp Prime Portal)

A close-up of the left rear of the turret on the M48A5, clearly showing the fan housing and the size of the turret rear stowage basket. Also visible is the rear of the rangefinder housing. (Erik Torp Prime Portal)

the chassis of the M48. All in all it has proved to be a real workhorse for the American Armoured Corps.

While we are looking at the variants it is worth noting the foreign versions too. The M48 was sold, or used as captured equipment, by many countries. Some used the tank straight from the box, while others made changes to suit their national requirements. Austria retired the last of her M48s sometime in the late 1980s but they still serve in an abstract way in that the hulls were scrapped but the turrets were retained and mounted on pillboxes along her borders – creating a quick and cheap defensive perimeter. Belgium no longer has any M48s, relying on Leopards. The former Federal Republic of Germany received large quantities of both M47s and M48s to equip the fledgling Bundeswehr. Some were categorized as M48A2GA2s which were M48A2s fitted with the 105mm gun, with local modifications provided by Wegmann and Company. As the German republic withdrew their M48s they were often sold or passed on to other NATO nations for another lease on life. Greece received around 500 M48s. The Greeks converted the tanks to diesel, but like most others they are no longer in front-line service.

Iran has had to make its own repairs and modifications to the M48. Due to the international arms embargo spares and other equipment are no longer available. Often the Iranians will exhibit a 'new' MBT which is clearly a M48 with add-ons. The most prolific user and modifier of the tanks has been Israel, which believes that nothing should be wasted and once a tank had passed its useful life it will be converted into another type of AFV. The one feature that was quickly removed was the M1 cupola which, due to its restrictive design,

Top view of the rear half of the turret. For modellers, note the cast texture. (Erik Torp Prime Portal)

Three-quarter view of the M48A5. It shows the rounded edge join between the upper and lower glacis very well. (Erik Torp Prime Portal)

This M48A5 has just fired its licence-built British L7 105mm gun. Notice the subdued two-tone camouflage and the tightly packed camouflage net in the rear basket. This Greek tank has the British Chieftain-type multi-barrelled smoke dischargers fitted; one is visible on the front right of the turret with its canvas cover fitted.

Every tank crew's nightmare: throwing a track or bogging down. Both usually require a lot of hard work, trying to self-recover if bogged down. If the track has been thrown they can try driving back and forward as sometimes this will rest the track. If not, the track has to be broken, then re-aligned and joined up. Joining a split track is not easy even on a hard surface, on soft ground it is a mission. (Carl Tarrant M48 Appreciation Society)

A Greek M48A5 fitted with a dozer blade is making good time down a dusty road. It has a .50-calibre Browning machine gun, and the loader has what appears to be a German 7.62mm machine gun. (Sotris Kon)

was blamed by the Israelis for many of their commander casualties. Commanders would have to expose themselves from the cupola to see, thus becoming targets. From this came the low-profile Urdan cupola. In battle, the Israeli M48s were usually able to take on the Egyptian T-55s and T-62s with no problem. The various modifications employed by the Israelis are numerous but include the use of plenty of turret-mounted machine guns.

Jordan was another user of the M48 which initially caused problems for the Israelis as it was felt blue-on-blue contact could easily happen. They were not employed on the Jordanian front line as a result. Other users include Morocco, Norway, Portugal, South Korea – who often fitted bazooka plates similar to those seen on Centurion and Chieftain – Spain, Taiwan, Thailand

and Turkey, who received many of the old German tanks that had been replaced.

Another user, who was also the second largest combat user outside the United States, was Pakistan. They were pitched against the Centurions and M4 Shermans of the Indian Army. They did not fare so well against the older tanks even though they were superior to the elderly Shermans. The Centurion was a much tougher proposition; although older, it was a very rugged tank. The losses for the Pakistanis were down to their poor handling and tactical awareness. The crews struggled with the M48 fire-control equipment and the lack of necessary skills to employ armoured infantry to protect their flanks cost them dearly. The M48 was not as capable in boggy ground as the Centurion which can go virtually anywhere. Once they got bogged down they were prey to tank-killing teams.

One assumes these rather damp Turkish tank soldiers are simply waiting for a parade to start and are not contemplating a heist. (Military Vehicles)

M48 Patton Specialist Variants

The M48 hull provided the basis for several variants, which is quite normal in tank development. If you have a hull that has proved sound and fits the requirements of the special variant you wish to build, it makes sense to utilize it. One such version was the M48 Armoured Vehicle Launched Bridge (AVLB). One problem armies have when advancing is that opposing forces will do everything to slow them down. One obvious way to do this is to blow transport bridges. In the days of the First World War this was recognized and some of the British tanks were adapted to carry bridges to help span the gap. Another method of filling small gaps was for tanks to carry rolled brushwood fascines to be dropped into the gap. This worked very well and is still employed today, although plastic pipes have replaced the brushwood.

To span something bigger the AVLB was developed, utilizing the hull of a M48 as a scissor bridge – so called because it folded in half as opposed to a single span bridge. This was designed along with its associated hydraulic equipment and was fitted to the M48. By 1958 the equipment was standardized. The M48 had its turret removed and a crew of two was required to operate it. In use the AVLB would approach the obstacle – M48 gun tanks would be to

its rear protecting it. Once in position the system would start to launch the bridge, a triangular structure rotated through 90 degrees, raising the bridge to the vertical position. It also took the weight of the bridge from the chassis. As the bridge left the vertical position the halves started to move apart, until the whole bridge was extend nearly flat. At this point the bridge would be lowered. An ejection cylinder, located in the launching arm, then pushed the bridge forward from the arm, around seven to eight inches, and the AVLB would back away to disengage itself from the bridge. Once clear, the supporting armour could cross, followed shortly after by the AVLB so it would be ready to collect the bridge and carry on the advance. This was the great advantage the AVLB had over a conventionally laid engineer's bridge: it was easy to install and remove. The M48 could utilize two different lengths of bridge, one was 19.2m (63ft) while the second was 13m (43ft). In practice, the larger bridge was the most commonly used as it was found it could bridge nearly 58.5 percent of expected obstacles.

Early AVLBs used M48 and M48A1 chassis and later standardized on M48A2s. No attempt was made to fit a diesel chassis until 1976, which proved cheaper than

A M48A2C AVLB showing the bridge-launch profile. As this is an exhibit vehicle, the forward part of the bridge has been adjusted to rest on the ground for safety purposes. This does shows how a really long-span bridge can be laid without too much height compromising the location. (Nikos Bresta M48 Appreciation Society)

The rear end of the M48 AVLB showing how the bridge was supported by the bar running across the rear hull plate. As with all AVLBs, if a mechanical problem occurs, it can be a bit of a problem to get to the engine compartment. Unless an auxiliary power system is available the bridge may well have to be removed by a crane. (Prime Portal)

A profile of the M48 AVLB in its travel configuration. It shows that although quite a large piece of equipment, it is actually quite compact. However, once the British deployed the Chieftain AVLB it dwarfed the M48. (Prime Portal)

converting M60 hulls to AVLB standards. M48 AVLBs were supplied to other users such as Israel, the former West Germany and the Netherlands. The latter was not a user of the M48 but adapted the bridge components to their Mk 5 Centurions in preference to the Centurion-based AVLB. The main reason for this was that the Centurion's bridge was a single-span 12.2m (40ft) one and, as it was launched, it produced a 12.2m-high profile, which the scissors bridge did not.

During the Second World War most nations used, in one form or another, the flamethrower. Mostly this was used in a man-pack version, and the Americans found it very useful in dislodging Japanese defenders as they island hopped across the Pacific. The British developed what was probably the most fearsome of the flamethrowers. It is reported that the mere suggestion that these flamethrowers were in the location was sufficient to make many German troops surrender. The British took the hull of the Churchill tank, removed the bow gunner's machine gun and replaced it with a flamethrower head. Pipes ran under the hull and connected to a two-wheeled trailer that contained the flammable fluid and propellant. The resulting combination was known as the Crocodile. The trailer held 1,800 litres (400 gallons) of flame fuel and could project it over a distance 110m (120 yards). Far beyond the range of the man pack, and it still had its turret-mounted 75mm gun and Besa machine gun. While the Americans appreciated the use of this type of equipment, and several local attempts were produced, at the end of the war the United States Army did not have a flamethrower tank in its inventory.

Development was carried on but very much at snail's pace as it was not thought a requirement existed for one. Then came the Korean War. Work focussed mainly on the elderly M4 and M26 chassis but these were becoming obsolete and needed replacement. In 1955 the T67 was born. Using the M48 it was designed to look like a conventional gun tank, partly so that it would not draw fire on itself. The disguise was not difficult to achieve as they were identical unless the enemy got closer than 50 yards. The 90mm gun was replaced by the E23-30R1 flamethrower which was supplied with 378 gallons of fuel. Unlike the Crocodile all this was carried on board the tank. A range of 150–220 yards could be achieved with a maximum burn time of 60 seconds, although that would be under ideal conditions, and as war is never fought under ideal conditions, the usual range would be 100 yards. The M67A1 used the hull of the M48A2 and was fitted with the M7A1-6 flamethrower. This was the version used by the United States Army. The M67 and M67A2 were exclusively used by the Marine Corps. Flamethrowers are double-edged weapons in that they are good for shock effect, but as a weapon, it

A close-up picture of the launch gear for a M48 Armoured Vehicle Launched Bridge (AVLB). The large triangular portion is lowered to the ground by the ram behind it, this give support and a firm footing for the bridge to be launched. Note also at the bottom of the picture the British Chieftain-style smoke-grenade launcher shielded by its canvas cover. (Jeff Nelson Prime Portal)

Close-up picture of the main hydraulic ram on the M48AVLB. (Prime Portal)

A bit of 'pull me push me': either the tank is pulling the tractor or vice versa. Note how the commander is using his hatch as a seat while using the .50-calibre Browning, mounted on the M1 cupola roof, although the cupola-mounted gun is just visible. (Max Resfault)

The M67 flamethrower, based on the M48 tank, showing just how effective the flame can be. It is said that when the Germans learnt that British Crocodile flamethrowers were in the area, they surrendered. (M48 Appreciation Society)

are inaccurate, the fuel is limited and once used, they are of no use and must return to be refuelled. The Churchill could still use its main gun, although as the Crocodiles were high-value equipment, they would only use it as a last resort. Eventually M113 Armoured Personnel Carriers were fitted with flamethrowers and the M67A1 was removed from the army inventory along with the Marine versions.

No matter how useful and how well maintained a tank is there will always be occasions when it needs help. It could have a seized engine, it could have run over a mine, broken a track or a host of other problems. The options are: abandon the tank and walk, which is not really an option, or wait for the battlefield version of the automobile recovery services to turn up. At individual troop level, at least in the British Army, recovery is taught, as some situations could be resolved using the remaining tanks in the troop. Hence the reason why both Challenger 1 and 2 carry recovery bars and shackles. Troop recovery is a good idea as each squadron would only have one recovery vehicle.

If all else fails then the specialized recovery vehicle would have to be called to attend the 'casualty'. The United States Army, like the British and most major tank-using countries, base their recovery vehicles on the hull of the current main battle tank, although during the Gulf War, 1990–1 British forces were using three generations of armoured recovery vehicles. The recovery of battlefield casualties is most important, as the allies learnt in the to-and-fro war in North Africa. Although a tank may have been hit, and the crew killed or injured, nine times out of ten it can be repaired and sent back into service. In the United States Army the project for a medium to heavy tank recovery vehicle was started in 1954. It was known as the T88 and as far as possible it utilized the components from the M48 series which, at the time, was the current American medium tank.

However, as in all projects, opinions vary, and it was decided that since the trials of the T95 tanks were going well, it would be the new medium tank to replace M48. If these opinions had been heeded

The M88 in this image is using its blade to dig in to provide support when winching a stranded vehicle. It is not unusual for the winching vehicle to be pulled toward the casualty. (Toadman Images)

The M88 in action in Vietnam easily lifts a damaged M113 APC using its A-frame jib to lower the casualty onto a loader for return to a repair area. (Unknown)

The M88 being used to either fit or remove a Pearson full-width mine plough from an American Assault Breaker Vehicle, which is based on the M1 Abrams main battle tank. (Marin Wright)

all the development work would have been lost. The designers and production company stood fast and insisted that the T-88 stay as it was. Luckily they triumphed and the T95 tank never entered production. The design focussed on the recovery crew having good visibility for all recovery purposes, and for a hull design that would allow good approaches to the casualty if it was required to remove a major assembly. The design provided space for recovery equipment – winches were a higher priority than ballistic protection as, although a recovery vehicle may go near the front line it would not expect to be fighting, so armour can be lower. Armour is usually against machine-gun fire and shell fragments. Two winches were fitted, with the main winch having a pull of 40,823kg (90,000lb) and the secondary winch 5,670kg (12,500lb). The secondary winch was to be used in conjunction with an A frame that could be erected on the front of the vehicle. This could be used for a variety of tasks: when the A frame was in use a front-mounted blade, similar to a dozer blade, could be lowered to aid stability. Although it looked like a dozer blade, and could be used as one in emergencies, its primary role was to support the tank when the jib was in use.

It is obvious that certain tasks, such as erecting and using the A-frame jib, meant the recovery crews had to leave the protection of the armoured recovery vehicle. Operating the jib or fastening tow bars or ropes to dead tanks put them at risk. To try and alleviate this trials were carried out on remote couplings that would allow the recovery vehicle to drive up, and by remote control, attach the couplings before driving away. While admirable in theory, there were a host of problems that meant the dead vehicle could not be moved even if it was coupled up – if there was track and road wheel damage it would severely restrict the towing capacity. Eventually, although two different systems were trialled, neither was taken into service. During the first Gulf War the British Royal Electrical and Mechanical Engineers (REME) took their Challenger-based recovery vehicle right into the heart of an incident. The crew had to climb out to cut track damage and attach winch ropes, all the time under enemy fire, although closely supported by other Challenger tanks.

The T88 proved that it could do all that was asked of it, so on 19 February 1959 it was officially classified as the M88 recovery vehicle. The hull of the M88 was a single large casting, in which the commander and driver sat side by side, leaving a roomy area for equipment and other crew members behind them. The commander's cupola was equipped with a simple pintle mount for a .50-calibre Browning machine gun. The A-frame jib was operated on the M88 by two schedule B hydraulic cylinders that were controlled from inside the vehicle. When not in use it was swung back until it lay flat on the rear decks. Usually it was left fully rigged so it was always ready for use.

The original M88 produced from 1960–4 used the Continental petrol engine and a 10hp auxiliary engine. During the upgrade to M88A1 the engine was replaced with a Continental diesel engine, and the auxiliary was changed to diesel too. The M88 and M88A1 were designated medium recovery vehicles. However, the M88A2, which is slightly bigger than the previous two vehicles, is classed as a heavy recovery vehicle. Although they all look the same, the M88A2 is much heavier, weighing in at 70 tons compared with the 56 tons of the previous two. The M88A2 has addressed some of the issues of its predecessors in that it has upgrade-armour packages that include armoured skirting plates, and add-on panels. The M88 has no NBC protection, but both the M88A1 and the M88A2 are equipped with these defences. With the introduction of the M1 Abrams it was found that it would take two M88A1s to tow a dead M1. The decision to upgrade the vehicle to M88A2 standards was taken in 1991. The vehicle is still in service with American forces and with at least 23 other countries' armies.

One of the problems that armoured forces have, and have had since aircraft became more than just a novelty, is the threat of air attack. One only has to see the devastation wrought by Hawker Typhoons and other aircraft on the retreating German Army in the Second World War. It is noteworthy that the Germans fielded some of the best anti-aircraft equipment during that conflict and still suffered huge losses. That threat has not gone away, if anything it has got worse, especially with the introduction of helicopters like the Apache. This has led to calls from some that 'the tank is dead'. The truth is, it is not, tanks will be roaming battlefields for a while yet. Even today, mobile anti-aircraft defence does not seem a high priority. So what was it like in the days of our M48? For the American forces, and to some extent their allies, it was not a high priority since the Allies ruled the skies. At the end of the war the Americans were left with half-tracks mounting quadruple .50-calibre Brownings and the M19 that was fitted with twin 40mm Bofors guns. They worked well, and were popular with the crews and supporting infantry, because they could put down a lot of suppressive fire in a short time, as the air threat was still considered low. However, they lacked several characteristics that would make them ideal partners for the armoured formations. Although they were not MBTs they were still expected to be fairly near the front line, so the maximum of firepower, mobility and protection needed to be applied. These three requirements are the basis for all armour design no matter what country. Although they can be in an order of preference that suits the country in question. The M19 and half-tracks had

It is common to build a recovery vehicle based on the chassis of your current battle tank. For the M48 that spawned the M88 Armoured Recovery Vehicle. This went through several versions with the M88A2 being the latest. It has picked up the name Hercules. (Toadman Images)

The latest variant of the M88, known as Hercules, has many modifications to enable it to continue service for many years. Modifications include a better jib, winches, transmission and armour. The name is an acronym of Heavy Equipment Recovery Combat Utility Lift and Evacuation System. (Wiki Commons)

the firepower but lacked sufficient mobility to keep up with the ever-increasing speeds across country of modern armour. They also lacked protection, both utilized open fighting positions, and this was made even worse as the chemical element crept onto the battlefield.

The vehicle to replace both of these was the M42 Duster. Based on the M24 Chaffee light tank, it was equipped with twin 40mm Bofors in an open-top turret. When deployed to Vietnam it was well liked for the awesome amount of firepower it could lay down. However, it was no nearer finding a solution. As no credible air threat had materialized during Vietnam or Korea, air defence again took a back seat. Other nations more or less followed American doctrine, apart from the British who did not even do that. The British toyed with various options in the following years but even now have no dedicated air-defence vehicle. The introduction of the Soviet ZSU 57/2 and ZSU 23/4 and the German Gepard gave the

The M42 Duster was the other main vehicle used alongside the M48 in Vietnam for defending the camp perimeters. Armed with twin 40mm Bofors guns it could put down quite a substantial rate of fire. (Weichado Chen Prime Portal)

The ill-fated M247 Sergeant York air-defence system based on the M48 hull. A brilliant concept that failed because the equipment did not live up to the claims made by the manufacturers. It is thought that around seven vehicles remain in various locations in the United States. (Brent Sauer Prime Portal)

This is an Israeli version of the mine roller; the rollers are of substantial construction. Note that there are several mountings for machine guns on top of the Magach turret. (Wiki Commons)

Americans the motivation to re-examine air defence. The ZSU 23/4 Shilka gave the Soviets a head start and was an impressive weapon. Four 23mm cannon in a fully enclosed radar-controlled turret, made it a very formidable weapon. A Tornado pilot and veteran of the Gulf War said the one thing they feared in that conflict was coming in range of the ZSU. The German Gepard mounted twin 35mm cannons in a fully enclosed radar-controlled turret mounted on a Leopard tank chassis.

The American reaction was to conduct various programmes and fit the M61 Vulcan cannon onto the chassis of the M113, and the MIM-72 Chaparral, which had the combination of Sidewinder missiles on the ubiquitous M113. Due to various issues the weapons were never really successful so the search went on. The resulting vehicle was based on the M48 chassis and utilized many of the shelf components in an effort to keep the cost down.

On 13 January 1978, General Dynamics and Ford were given development contracts for one prototype each, of their designs for the new weapon, designated XM246 and XM247 respectively. They were to be delivered to Fort Bliss in June 1980. On schedule, both companies delivered their prototypes to the North McGregor Test Facility and head-to-head testing began. They shot down two F-86 Sabre fighters, five UH-1 Huey helicopters and twenty-one smaller drones. Ford's use of the well-used 40mm Bofors caused controversy and claims of political bias: Ford had connections to Bofors. The General Dynamics version used the European standard 35mm. In the end Ford won the contract despite General Dynamics having consistently out shot it.

Problems started to appear almost before the ink was dry on the contract. The tracking radar had difficulty in distinguishing a helicopter from a tree; one can only visualize the amount of trees shot down during the trials. If the guns was at maximum elevation the barrels interfered with the radar line of sight and confused it even more, and the reaction times were classed as too slow. Not surprisingly a major problem was that the use of the 30-year-old M48 chassis, with the new 20-ton turret, meant the vehicle had trouble keeping pace with the newer M1 and M2: the vehicles it was meant to protect. During a demonstration to various senior officers from both the United States and the United Kingdom, the vehicle systems, once activated, decided the viewing stand was a suitable target and traversed the guns onto it. The resulting melee that this conjures up would be amusing if it was not so serious. When it did fire things got even worse: it decided the aerial targets were 300 metres in front of the vehicle on the ground. The demonstration ended in farce and was obviously not classified a success. An amusing footnote to that day was a comment made by a Ford representative;

A posed picture: if the tank was mine clearing the commander certainly would not be sitting up like he is. It can be seen from the picture just how the mine roller is articulated so it can follow the contours of the ground. This is a very slow-moving task and the tank would probably be covered by overwatch tanks. (M48 Appreciation Society)

A very different variant of the M48 was proposed and several were built by the Wegmann Company of Germany; It was based on the German M48A2GA2. The idea was to enable the M48 to hold its own against the more modern battle tanks coming into service. It was equipped with a modular armour package – which changed its shape totally – new power drives for the turret, main armament stabilization and a new engine and transmission. Five were built and were aimed at those who already had M48s, because plentiful supplies of ex-Cold War tanks were available then. It was, however, the ultimate M48 upgrade. (M48 Appreciation Society)

A very garishly decorated M48 fitted with the M8 dozer-blade kit in Vietnam. The blade was of great use in Vietnam as it allowed scrapes to be dug very quickly, it also cleared trees and vegetation around fire bases. (flickriver)

he blamed the issues on the vehicle being washed down prior to the demonstration. Fifty vehicles, now known as the M247 Sergeant York – one of Americas most decorated heroes from the First World War – had been built when the project was finally, and probably with great relief, cancelled in August 1985. The majority of the M247s were expended on ranges, although at least three have survived. A sad end to a vehicle named after a brave man, and probably the least successful of the conversions based on the M48 hull.

Mines are one of the weapons that tank crews fear. They are cheap and quickly laid but can easily immobilize or even destroy a tank, as they attack the tank's weak spot: the hull bottom. A lot of work was done by the Americans on mine warfare and some impressively named, if not useful, equipment was produced, with names like High Herman and Larruping Lou. They can be simply described as heavy and light mine-clearing equipment. Most of the designed equipment was based on the use of front-mounted heavy (21-tons) rollers that were pushed into a suspected mined area. It was hoped that the weight would be enough to detonate any mines. Today the most common method seems to be the full-width mine plough.

M48 was also able to be fitted with a hydraulically operated dozer blade, the one used was the M8 dozer kit. Although they were widely used in Vietnam, there seems to be little use for them after that war. One unusual variant of the M48 was used to trial the 152mm Shillelagh gun-launched guided missile. It was fitted to a heavily modified M48. Once the trials were complete, this most unusual vehicle in the M48 series, was destroyed as a range target: a loss indeed.

These are the major variants built using the M48, but like all tests and trials

Top view of the M48A1 fitted with the M8 plough during one of the many crash outs in West Germany during the early days of the Cold War. This is located near the famous Checkpoint Charlie. (Anne Marie Skurda M48 Appreciation Society)

M48 Patton in Action

there will be many more one-offs that will probably never see the light of day.

The M48 has seen its fair share of combat since its introduction, with the United States Army and foreign users. Probably the most enthusiastic user was the Israeli Defence Forces. Originally the American government had banned the sale of M48s to Israel, but eventually relented and slowly started to supply them with the tanks. The Israelis have never been shy to modify equipment they have bought to suit their particular needs. An example is the British Centurion. Although an admirable fighting machine, it was not really up to the long dessert battles that would be fought by Israel. Rather than discarding it, they changed the thirsty Meteor petrol engine for a diesel engine and made many other modifications that changed the Centurion into a superb machine. It fought with distinction in many of the wars that Israel has had to fight. The M48 was no exception to this practice of improvement. One of the first items the Israelis decided to replace was the 90mm gun. In its place they used the British L7 105mm gun; they felt this was better suited for engaging the ever-increasing amounts of Soviet T-54s that were being supplied to the Egyptian and Syrian armies. When Israel engaged in what became known as the Six Day War

in 1967, around 15–20 M48s had been converted: the equivalent of an Israeli tank company. Thus the remainder went to war virtually as they were when delivered from the United States.

Initially the Israelis refrained from deploying the M48 near the Jordanian border because both sides used the tank and confusion could lead to a blue-on-blue incident. The M48 was always going to be compared to the British Centurion; overall they came out fairly evenly matched. The M48 was found to be easier to maintain and had better armour than the early Centurions (later marks soon rectified this deficiency). One feature that was loathed by the Israeli tank crews was the M1 cupola, which we have seen was not popular anywhere. This led to the locally developed Urdan cupola which was also adopted by the United States. Overall the M48 was very successful in combat during the Six Day War. One battalion, commanded by Colonel Uri Barron, was involved in heavy fighting around the area known as Rafah Junction. During this attack they managed to destroy at least a dozen T-34/85s and 15 JS3 M heavy tanks, all of which were in well-prepared defensive positions. The M48 was also deployed in the fighting around Jiradi. This was very hard fighting and several tanks were lost to well-prepared minefields and well-sighted and dug in anti-tank weapons.

The next major conflict that the Israeli nation had to contend with was the surprise attack by the Arab nations on Yom Kippur in 1973, the holiest day of prayer and atonement. The state of alertness was low and the initial gains by the Arab forces great. The United States policy on supplying military equipment to Israel by now had changed and Israel had received 900 more M48s and several hundred M60s. Many of these M48s were fitted with the AVDS diesel engines and the licence-built British L7 105mm gun, the M68. This eased the modification work that would need to be done by the Israelis. One programme that they had instigated was the replacement of the M1 cupola with the Urdan version.

M48s were deployed to the Sinai areas while the Centurions were in the Golan Heights. Although the M48 was able to engage the T-55 and the newly arrived T-62, initial losses were high because the Israelis had rushed armour to the various fronts, mostly without any infantry support. This proved fatal once the Egyptian forces were found to be using the Soviet man-portable anti-tank missile known as the Sagger, or the 'suitcase missile' because it could be packed into a stowage box the size of a suitcase. The use of the RPG-7s also caused causalities. Once the infantry forces caught up the grenade launchers' effectiveness was negated. After the losses of M48s in the Six Day War, tank commanders had been trained to operate fully closed down. However, this always reduces the visibility of the tank commander and thus it was easier for the tank-hunting parties to succeed. The policy soon changed and more turret-mounted machine guns appeared and were used to provide speculative fire into likely tank-hunting team positions.

During the war Israeli forces using M48 tanks took part in what was one of the biggest confrontations: the Battle of Chinese Farm. This took place from 15–18 October 1973. The battle involved the Egyptian 21st Armoured Division (136 tanks) and the Israeli 143rd and 162nd armoured divisions (more than 300 tanks). The battle ended with an Israeli victory, but both sides lost a huge number of tanks in this battle. On the night of 15/16 October the Israeli 14th Brigade of the 143rd Division lost 70 tanks out of 97. Between the 16th at 0900 and the 17th at 1400 the Israeli 143rd and 162nd divisions had lost 96 tanks. As of 18 October the Egyptian 21st Armoured Division had no more than 40 tanks remaining of 136 available at the start of the battle. The loss of life and equipment on both sides was tremendous but the Arab forces suffered the most once the Israeli counterattack crossed the canal and advanced, cutting off the Egyptian 3rd Army and totally surrounding it. International pressure was now being felt and on 25 October a ceasefire was signed. Israel had

Israeli Magach, a version of the M48 series. Note the .50-calibre Browning located above the mantlet. This is used as a ranging gun and is fired remotely by means of a cable attachment. (Phototrain)

This picture shows a typically equipped Magach in the very distinctive Israeli paint scheme. This vehicle is located at the Littlefield Foundation Museum, Palo Alto, USA. (Toadman photos)

lost around 900 tanks with many of those being M48s. Although not a modern tank, the M48 performed exceptionally well in the hands of the Israeli tank crews, partly due to better training and logistic support. In service with the Israeli Defence Forces the M48 was known as the Magach, with the Magach 1, 2, 3 and 5 based on the M48 while the 6 and 7 are based on the M60 series.

It was at first thought that the jungles of Vietnam would be no place for armour, apart from light mobile vehicles like the M113 Armoured Personnel Carriers. However, there was soon a need and good use for heavier armour and the M48A3s landed at Danang in South Vietnam. Although this was not their first operational deployment; they had been used in July 1958 when United States Marine Corps' M48s were deployed to Lebanon as part of the peacekeeping force. There it saw no real fighting compared with what was to come in Vietnam. The first tanks were used by the Marines with the first army units arriving in 1965. These belonged to the 4th Cavalry Regiment. As already noted, the powers that be had little enthusiasm for the use of

Looking across the whole turret forward, the fume extractor on the 105mm can just be made out. Notice the height of the casting numbers, They are very prominent and do stand out. This view also shows the very limited view to the rear that the commander had compared to today's commander's stations with 360-degree periscopes and television cameras. (Erik Torp Prime Portal)

This shows the Israeli solution to the M1 cupola: get rid of it and fit your own. Note the low profile of the Urdan cupola, and the fitting of a .30-calibre Browning on it with a .50-calibre Browning on the mantlet. Note also the apparent lack of vision devices on the cupola and the track link stowage on the turret side. (Leicester Modellers Society)

A typical Vietnam scenario of the infantry hitching a ride to the front line. This was very common in the Soviet forces during the Second World War and during the Cold War. (M48 Appreciation Society)

tanks, but the experiences of the 4th Cav, as it was known, showed that they were useful in support of armoured infantry. Soon there were three army tank battalions serving at any one time along with M48s from armoured cavalry units.

Vietnam was an unconventional war, the likes of which was new to the United States. As such they had to adopt tactics for the infantry, which applied to the use of armour. This was close jungle terrain unlike the vast training areas or the plains of Germany. One use was for the tanks to provide perimeter fire support to a base. If the Viet Cong attacked, the tanks made good use of their canister rounds which were devastating to the Viet Cong caught in the open. That is exactly what the canister round had been envisaged for. The main enemy of the tank in Vietnam was not tanks which were a rarity, although the North Vietnamese Army did field PT76 light tanks. The threat came from mines which caused over 75 percent of tank casualties in Vietnam, and the use of light, hand-held anti-tank weapons such as the Soviet produced RPG-7 which could be employed by one soldier to devastating effect. Although no tank is designed for this type of warfare the M48 proved remarkably rugged, and although mine damage could be fatal, it was often only necessary to fix damaged parts and the tank would be fit once more. In an attempt to totally destroy tanks, aerial mines, which were considerably larger than their ground counterparts, were employed by the Viet Cong. If used correctly, they were more than capable of taking out a tank. In one incident a M48A3 hit one such mine and the resulting explosion tore the whole rear section off including the engine. Miraculously the crew survived. It was estimated that the mine used was in the region of 500lbs. In 1967 the American government came up with a plan that showed a real lack of understanding and was universally disliked by tank crews. They replaced the rugged and reliable M48 with the M551 Sheridan. The M551, due to its requirement to be air portable, was light on armour protection and very susceptible to major damage when hit by mines. In such events it was usually the driver who fared worst. Its lightness was also a disadvantage when trying to force its way through the dense jungle. It either did not have the power to do this or it led to quite serious damage. Its other major issue was its weapon. The M551 Sheridan had been designed to enable a tank killer to be air dropped into the forward battle area to give the troops a good tank-killing capability. To this end it was equipped with the M81/M81 Modified/M81E1 152mm gun/launcher, which fired both conventional ammunition and the MGM-51 Shillelagh guided anti-tank missile.

Not all things about the Sheridan, named after General Philip Henry Sheridan, a Union general in the American Civil War, were bad. It did not get stuck in the mud as often as the 52-ton M48 Patton tank, nor did it throw its track off as often. This alone was enough to win the tank crews' favour. Replacing a thrown track is hard enough on nice firm ground but in the muddy undulating ground of Vietnam, with the constant threat of enemy action, it must have been a nightmare. Its light weight, which had been seen as an issue, actually allowed it to have a high degree of manoeuvrability, and the gun proved an effective anti-personnel weapon when used with either the M657 HE shell or the M625 canister round which used thousands of flechettes as projectiles. These operate like canister rounds except instead of steel balls they were filled with little darts, making them more accurate. One thing that was never rectified was the unreliability of the engine. For example, 74 Sheridans were sent to Vietnam in February 1969, and three months later 16 of them had major mechanical faults. The issues with the gun launcher would never be totally rectified either. The major difference between the 90mm, 105mm and the 152mm gun launcher was that the first two used a fixed-brass case for the propelling charge. This meant the round was loaded as a single unit and the case sealed the breech. Once the round was fired in a M48 the loader could insert another round. However, in the Sheridan, due to the fact that air was used to clear the bore, the loader had to wait for the breech to open before very carefully loading the fragile rounds. It was said that a M48 could get nine rounds off while the M551 could manage only two in a minute. If rounds became separated from their charge the rule was, don't use that round. If in action, these were often allowed to remain on the turret floor. If the tank was hit by an anti-tank round this would cause a massive conflagration, and the total destruction of the vehicle, with the aluminium hull melting while the conventional steel turret remained intact.

Due to its size the Sheridan had to carry a lot of its spare small-arms ammunition strapped to the turret side. Conventional 152mm rounds were only used in Vietnam as there was just no need for the tank-busting capabilities of the Shillelagh missile.

Despite all the reports of doom and gloom, with deaths and wrecked vehicles, the Sheridan was very much appreciated by the infantry, who were desperate for direct fire support. This it could give, especially firing flechette rounds into massed ranks of attacking infantry. Throughout its service the Sheridan continued to suffer losses which rose considerably once the United States became embroiled in Cambodia. It is fair to say that the Sheridan was an innovative weapon system but used in the wrong theatre.

As we have seen, tank-versus-tank combat was not a common occurrence,

This M48 has paused in a muddy track somewhere in Vietnam. Notice the extra small-arms ammunition stacked on the catwalks on either side of the driver, and the markings on the searchlight cover. (M48 Appreciation Society)

This M48 Patton is in an overwatch position guarding a road in Vietnam. The earth embankment gives it some frontal protection. The commander's cupola is the version fitted with the riser block. Note the ammunition boxes on the front right wing. The crew looks fairly relaxed and ready for a long, boring spell of duty. (Wiki Commons)

This M48 is ploughing through the heavy and wet terrain in Vietnam, damage to the track guards can be seen. The loader is leaning out watching for any unseen obstacles; this, and the position of the commander, indicates that they are not in contact. (Martin Hargreaves)

This M48 in Vietnam is in a semi-dug-in position, ideal for static defensive work. Notice the artwork on the tanks and the rather bemused looks of the civilians going about their daily tasks. (M48 Appreciation Society)

The M67 flamethrower in action in Vietnam. Of interest is the little Rifle Multiple 106mm Self-propelled M50 or 'Ontos'. It mounted six 106mm recoilless rifles which, if required, could be fired in sequence to ensure a kill on target. Reloads were carried in a compartment below the main hull floor which could be an issue if hit by a mine as it was very lightly armoured. (Wiki Commons)

and as far as records go there was only one recorded tank fight. This took place between the regular forces of the North Vietnamese Army, equipped with the Soviet-built PT76 light tank and BTR 50 wheeled armoured personnel carriers, and American armoured forces. The NVA attacked the base at Ben Hut which was the base for a battery of 175mm artillery pieces which had been causing the Vietnamese lots of problems. The base was defended by M42 Dusters, with their twin 400mm Bofors guns, and a platoon of M48A3s. During the attack one PT76 was hit by a landmine and was disabled but kept firing. Although it was putting fire down the end result was going to be its destruction; a rule of armoured warfare is that you never stay in the same place for more than two rounds fired. If you do you're dead. Thus it was for the unfortunate PT76. One of the defending M48A3s used the PT76's muzzle flash as an aiming point and with its second round a High Explosive Anti-Tank (HEAT) round slammed into the PT76 and it immediately turned into a fireball. Soon after a second PT76 was destroyed and the attack fizzled out. The losses, apart from men to the North Vietnamese, were two PT76s and a BTR 50. Thus ended the only real tank-versus-tank action in Vietnam.

The only other occasion of armour versus armour was when a M728 combat-engineer tank – which was armoured with a 165mm bunker-busting gun, similar to that carried by the British Centurion engineer variant – came across a T-54 and fired a 165mm bunker-busting high explosive round at it, with the inevitable result. There were other occasions when the M48 proved itself, but single tank-on-tank actions were those mentioned. One attack by the North Vietnamese Army cost them nine PT76s and two T-54s while the 20th Tank Regiment managed to destroy 16 T-54s.

One variant of the M48 used in Vietnam was the M67A2 flamethrower. Although used in limited engagements it was still enough to deter local attacks. However, it was still hamstrung in that it had only 60 seconds' burn before needing refuelling. The M113, equipped with the same flame gun, could carry much more fuel and was preferred by the army. The M48 and its crew can feel quite rightly that they did their job in the difficult terrain they had to operate in. The M48 proved it was rugged and could take the punishment dished out to it.

The other major conflict that the M48 fought in was the battles between India and Pakistan. These were in fact the M48's first real taste of combat, although most reports of the actions fought between the two countries should be viewed judiciously in that they claimed more tanks destroyed than were proven. The first taste of battle came during 1965. We will only concern ourselves with the participation of the M48 during the war and not the reasons for it. The main tank used by the Indians was the British Centurion while Pakistan fielded versions of the M48. On 1 September 1965 the Pakistan Army advanced into the Chamb Sector in the hope of luring the Indian forces to engage them. If the Indians had done so they would have fought with the Pakistanis to their front and the River Chenab to their rear, which would have been a total disaster. Instead they launched a series of attacks aimed toward Lahore. They quickly advanced and by 6 September they had reached the Ichhogil Canal. However, the Pakistanis either held the bridges over it or destroyed those they did not control, thus halting the Indian advance for the moment. The Pakistanis attempted to advance along the area occupied by the Indians' left flank, hoping to trap them against the canal. The advance was slow because the Pakistanis had to deploy elaborate bridging procedures to cross the canal. M48s and M24 Chaffees, acting in a reconnaissance role, were ambushed by the Indians with more tanks lost in the flooded plains. All this activity indicated to the Indians what was coming and, since they occupied the advantageous ground, they withdrew to consider their next move. This included laying a trap for the advancing Pakistanis. No one at the time could have foreseen that the coming

This is the M551 Sheridan that was selected to replace the M48 Pattons in Vietnam. It can be seen that it is a much smaller vehicle armed with a 152mm gun/missile launcher. Although only conventional ammunition was used, an effective round used by the M551 was the flechette anti-personnel round. This one has the added armoured protection around the commander's cupola. (Greg Smith Prime Portal)

Above: A M48A2 smoulders after a 90mm canister round cooked off in the breech. (M48 Appreciation Society.)

Below: When it all goes badly wrong: the burnt-out hull of a Pakistani M48. The force of the explosion has popped the turret; this is a common occurrence on Russian-manufactured tanks, but as the picture shows, it can happen to anyone. (The Times of India)

battle would produce a tank-versus-tank conflict of a scale not seen since the Battle of Kursk on the Eastern Front during the Second World War.

The Indian armour was deployed in a horseshoe shape into which was hoped the advancing Pakistani armour would blunder and be destroyed. Up until 9 September the efforts of the Pakistanis had been lacklustre to say the least, as they remained stationary while awaiting the arrival of the remainder of its forces. Its commanders would make no move until they were in place. During this period they should have been at risk from the Indian Air Force, but their efforts were equally uninspiring. Their only major contribution was to destroy a supply echelon. This left many of the Pakistani M48s with 30 rounds to load for the main armament, hardly the amount you want when you are going to be fighting what they hoped would be a decisive battle. The ground over which the Pakistanis would

have to advance was very fertile and the crop of sugar cane was in full growth providing cover for troops. The next phase took place on 10 September when the Pakistani 5th Armoured Brigade was sent forward to attack. Things started to go wrong for the Pakistanis almost immediately because the Indian artillery and infantry were picking off the Pakistani Infantry with apparent ease. This left the M48s charging forward with little or no support, which is not a good plan in front of a well-emplaced enemy. They had little option but to advance through the high sugar cane, and with their infantry all but non-existent they become easy prey for the Indian tank crews and recoilless-rifle teams. As they advanced they were disturbing the sugar cane and the swaying thereof gave the Indian gunners a good indication of their targets. Very soon the defensive fire of the Indians began to take a toll on the M48s' advance, and began hitting them from both the front and the sides causing many casualties. One Pakistani regiment, in an attempt to complete its mission and carry the attack to the enemy, tried to outflank the Indian forces only to find itself stuck in a plain that had been flooded by the Indians in expectation of such a move. Those M48s that succeeded in extricating themselves from the morass the ground had become, reached what they thought would be the safety of firm ground. However, they found that Indian armour and artillery, dug in and well-hidden, suddenly opened up on the luckless Pakistani tanks who were quickly decimated without managing to destroy any Indian armour. Later in the day the Pakistani 4th Armoured Brigade was ordered to try and take the right flank but they fared no better than their 5th Armoured Brigade comrades. Again the Indians, with clear tactical thinking, had flooded the plains and the result was almost identical, with Pakistani tanks being picked off one by one by Indian armour and artillery.

Nightfall thankfully brought some respite for the Pakistanis. They had lost 97 tanks, mostly M48s, but also M47s. These figures become more awesome when you consider that the Indians claim to have lost only 12 tanks. If that figure is accurate it shows exactly what good defensive positions and intelligence can do, aided by the poor planning of the enemy. With this phase over the Indians now turned their attention to what they called Operation Nepal, to seize the road around Wazirabad. Their infantry managed to take the border which in turn alerted the Pakistanis as to what was happening. They sent urgent reinforcements which included around 135 tanks of mixed types including M47s, M48s, M36s and M4 Shermans. This battle went a little better for the Pakistanis and, although their air force did not manage to knock out any armour, it did destroy support echelons with valuable fuel and ammunition. As for the Pakistanis earlier, the ground gave indications of where the enemy armour was: the road the Indians used was dry and a large dust cloud followed them.

The Indians managed to advance as far as Phillaur but were forced back, losing 15 tanks in the process. For two days a stalemate existed with both sides taking stock of the situation. The next move was by Centurions that were quickly engaged by Pakistani tanks, supported by infantry anti-tank teams and their recoilless rifles. These engagements ran on for at least 12 hours, with the dust making it hard to distinguish one side from the other. At the end of the day the Indians proudly announce the destruction of over 65 Pakistani tanks, most of which were claimed to be M48s. Impressive figures, but the Pakistanis did not have that number of tanks in that area so the claim does not really stand up. However, the Pakistanis were again forced to withdraw. The next attacks took place on 13 September and

raged for two days. The finale took place when the Indian attack was broken up by the Pakistanis use of M48s and anti-tank teams firing Cobra anti-tank missiles. However, both sides were now feeling the strain and suffering heavy losses. From this date, until the ceasefire on 23 September, the majority of fighting was confined to artillery duels. An idea of the ferocity of the fighting was reported by a British journalist who visited soon after the ceasefire. Although the Indian Army was rapidly recovering, they counted 25 Centurions that had been hit and burnt out, 11 of these in an area no larger than 800 yards in width. The final accurate toll will probably never be known as both sides exaggerate their gains and downplay their losses. The Indians did however admit to losing 128 tanks in combat while Pakistan admitted to losing 168. This was the end of this round of Indo-Pakistani wars, and the M48 came away with a somewhat poor reputation which in retrospect is probably unfair. You can have the best tank in the world but if it is handled badly and thrown into hopeless situations and ground unsuited to combat it will take casualties, as was proved by the ill-conceived head-on charge into the trap at Asal Uttar. A lot of the M48 casualties were tanks that were simply abandoned by their crews. When the odds were equal the M48s manged to hold their own, as proved by their high success rate against the Centurions. Neither side showed great flair in the use of armour but when handling small units the success rate was far better. This then was the end for the M48 in combat in this region as it took no further part in the Indo-Pakistan War.

Combat use of the M48 by the Turkish Army in its invasion of Cyprus in 1974 was limited. There was not much opposition from the Greek forces defending the Island, and the tanks rolled on with one objective: Nicosia International Airport. The only thing standing between them and success was a troop of Mk 5 Ferret Scout cars, the super variant of this series, manned by soldiers of the 4th/7th Royal Dragoon Guards under the auspices of the United Nations. Each one was armed with four Swingfire anti-tank missiles. The ensuing conversation between the Turks and the British has entered regimental history. No matter what the truth is, the airport was never seized and the M48s stayed just outside the airport limits.

This then is the tale of the M48, a tank that has served in many countries and has seen its fair share of combat the world over. Some countries have made better use of it than others but it is fair to say that it has proved popular, and a rugged combat platform. Even today, in some smaller nations, it soldiers on in many modified forms: a tribute to its original designers and those who brought it into service. Although many called its replacement, the M60 a Patton tank, the M48 was the last to officially be given that name. A tank befitting a great general.